Dan Meinertzhagen, R. P Hornby

Bird Life in an Arctic Spring

The diaries of Dan Meinertzhagen and R. P. Hornby

Dan Meinertzhagen, R. P Hornby

Bird Life in an Arctic Spring
The diaries of Dan Meinertzhagen and R. P. Hornby

ISBN/EAN: 9783337095338

Printed in Europe, USA, Canada, Australia, Japan

Cover: Foto ©Andreas Hilbeck / pixelio.de

More available books at **www.hansebooks.com**

BIRD LIFE

IN AN

ARCTIC SPRING.

THE DIARIES OF

DAN MEINERTZHAGEN

AND

R. P. HORNBY.

LONDON:
PUBLISHED AT THE OFFICES OF "COUNTRY LIFE,"
20, TAVISTOCK STREET, LONDON, W.C.
1899.

DAN MEINERTZHAGEN.

DAN MEINERTZHAGEN'S DIARY.

(*1897.*) *March 29th.*—Left London by 11.30 train for Newcastle, with R. P. Hornby, for a bird-nesting expedition in Lapland; Hornby going chiefly for the fishing. We took with us:

1 small portmanteau containing clothes for the journey.

1 bag containing for each a change of clothes, 1 extra shirt each, 1 extra vest, 2 pairs of socks, an extra pair of boots, and brushes, etc.

2 large tin boxes containing provisions, medicine, rugs, books, etc.

2 gun cases.

3 boxes of cartridges, containing altogether about 1000 cartridges.

1 box containing tin boxes for packing eggs.

1 box containing methylated spirit in jars.

1 fishing basket containing knives, telescope, etc.

1 box containing rods.

We arrived at Newcastle about four in the morning and slept there.

March 30th. — We went to the Hancock Museum in this town, and I don't think I've ever been fascinated so much by stuffed birds as I have been to-day. The Falcons were particularly good. We also saw there the collection of Bewick's wood-cuts, and some original drawings by him. The boat leaves from North Shields at six o'clock in the afternoon.

April 1st.—Arrived in Bergen this morning in beautiful weather, but after a rough passage, very hungry, since we both had eaten nothing after leaving Shields; and what we ate there didn't last us long. I don't think I ever had a worse 36 hours in my life. Bergen is a large town, larger than Trondhjem, but I don't like the shops so much. We listened to the music in the gardens there for the greater part of the morning. We saw the first Eider Ducks coming up the fiord. In the evening we went to the Eldorado Music Hall, and left by the "Olaf Kyrre"—a boat in which I had been to Hammerfest two years ago—at 12 o'clock at night.

April 2nd.—To-day we have both got our sea-legs, but the weather is beastly, snowing and blowing, and the hills all around Bergen are covered with snow. Passed Aalesund, and in the night, Molde.

D.M.

A BIT OF NORWEGIAN COAST.

April 3rd.—A lovely day, but the sea still rough, and a good wind blowing. In the bit of open sea before Hitteren, I saw a whale, and the Captain told me two were seen that day. By Hitteren we saw Cormorants, Grey Crows, Starlings, Fieldfares, Black Guillemots, Eiders, and Long-tailed Ducks. This is the first time I have seen Long-tailed Ducks alive, and the first time Eiders in breeding plumage. The Long-tailed Ducks were in little parties of seven or eight, and much wilder than the Eiders. The plumage of the male Eider in breeding time is peculiar, since it is light above and darker below. This is the only bird I know in which the colours are so placed. Sitting on the rocks, which in winter and at Easter are covered with patches of snow, they would be very difficult to see—*protective mimicry* !—We arrived at Trondhjem in the evening.

April 4th.—We had intended to buy furs at Brunn's, in Trondhjem, yesterday, but we arrived late and the shops were closed ; so we went straight on board the "Vesteraalia" which was to start at eight o'clock this morning for Tromsö. To-day was very fine, and we passed Beian about ten, which is a small fishing village about 20 miles from Trondhjem at the mouth of the fiord; it lies very low, and is surrounded by lots of low rocks, and lying on the water between these were hundreds of Eiders and Long-tailed Ducks, and also we passed here a large flock of Velvet Scoters, and saw some porpoises; other birds we saw on the journey were Oyster Catchers, Puffins, common Guillemot, Raven, Gannet, Glaucous Gulls, and a Sea Eagle which was soaring, in the sunshine, over the ship. We saw its white tail very plainly in the sunshine when it turned away.

April 5th.—Still fine. We reach Bodö about mid-day. Just outside a young Sea Eagle was flopping about on the rocks within 20 yards of the ship, mobbed by the Grey Crows. In the afternoon there were about six hours of open sea, which we thoroughly enjoyed. We saw the Lofoten Islands when about 40 miles off, covered with snow, and looking like clouds on the horizon. We reached Svolvar about seven, and the sun was setting behind the islands and looked splendid; in fact, I don't think I ever saw a prettier and more imposing sunset. The fishermen here had caught two million cod during the few preceding days, and there was consequently a "beano" going on. Nearly all were drunk, and the place reeked of fish. Two men, father and son, who were carried on board blind drunk, were put with the luggage for Tromsö. We passed the Arctic Circle in the open sea, and when we went up on deck in the evening, saw the Aurora. The air was very cold. I had no idea the Aurora flashed about so over the sky : I thought it was almost stationary. We passed a most peculiar looking mountain to-day, something like this—

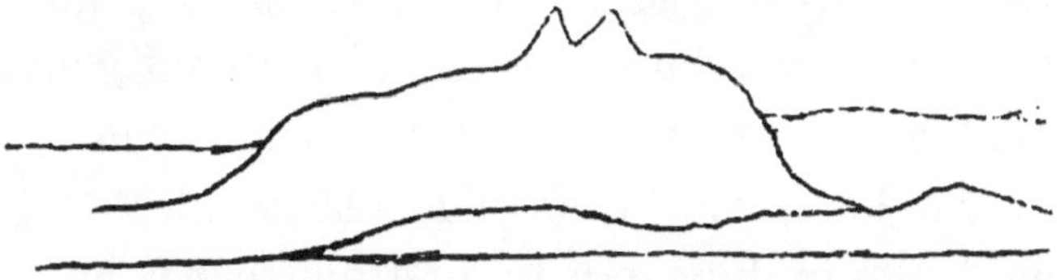

It looked as if a glacier had once passed over it, and rounding off most of it, had left the two highest peaks.

Tromso, April 6th.—Everybody is sledging about the streets here with bells on the sledges, and the whole place sounds to me what I imagine St. Petersburg to be. The captain of our steamer, Herr Neilsen, a very pleasant fellow, introduced us to a Herr Harald Hansen last night, who promised to give us help in Tromsö in buying our things, and showing us about. We saw another Sea Eagle this morning and some King Eiders. We arrived at Tromsö mid-day, and were really quite sorry to leave the boat and the captain. With the help of

Hansen we engaged a guide to take us to Muonioniska on Saturday, and also made arrangements for Bob to go out shooting to-morrow. In the evening we tried to get leave to shoot each a pair of Eider Ducks, but failed to get it. We also went to see a Captain Schlosshauer on his steamer "Glenmore," lying in the harbour. He is going in July to the Jenesei to trade, and coming back by sledge through Petersburg. He is a dear old gentleman who has travelled a lot, and been long in England, and I should dearly like to go with him in July, but I am afraid that is only a dream. We are staying at the Grand Hotel here, which is fairly comfortable, but no one speaks English, and we can't speak Norse. Six kr. a day each.

April 7th.—Bob went out shooting to-day in the fiord north of the town, and got one Eider Drake and two Ducks, two King Eider Drakes, and a Raven. After a lot of trouble and talking I got the Chief of Police here to give him leave to kill two pair of Eiders. They are protected by law. Bob shot some Long-tailed Ducks but failed to pick them up; he also had a shot at some Black Guillemot. He says he saw three White Falcons which rose about 80 yards in front of him; but the snow was so thick he could not follow them. His birds are being skinned by the Museum bird stuffer. I saw the Museum to-day. The two most interesting objects are a musk-ox from Greenland, and a cross between a Willow Grouse and a Blackcock, the only one known.

I bought the furs to-day. For each of us, 1 fur cap, 1 fur coat, 1 pair of fur boots reaching above the knee, 1 pair of plain reindeer leather boots with soles for wet weather. These cost 90 kr. the set, and we bought them at Hansen's in the town here.

I also bought for the journey—

	kr.	
1 box of oatmeal biscuits -	6	57
1 tin of Liebig . -	2	40
1 malet of Coffee - -	4	0
1 small packet of salt -	0	20
1 ,, ,, cooking	1	40
2 kilos dried vegetables -	3	60
	18	37
1 large ham (pig) - -	16	0
1 sausage - - -	2	0
	18	0

1 kettle, 3 plates, 3 cups, and 3 pairs of snow spectacles.

I was horrified to find that *all* the tobacco I brought from England had turned mouldy, and had to buy some more here, which is very good and cheap. I only paid 11 kr. for 4 lbs. of the best, and I think they are larger than English pounds, for the parcel containing the tobacco is as big as my body.

Our future guide, whose full name is Isak Gustav Eriksen, is a half-bred Finn, his mother being a Swede.

I heard yesterday a cooing noise coming from the direction of the King Eiders, and Bob who saw them near to-day, says the males fight for the females, and it is then that they make this peculiar note. He says the male swims about in front of the female, stretching his neck out, and assuming various attitudes, cooing all the while, until another male comes up and shows fight, and the victor then begins cooing again. The wind is rising and I'm afraid we shall not be able to go out in a boat to-morrow.

Tromsö, April 8th.—To-day it is blowing a gale and our fisherman-hunter came and told us it was useless going out. I am getting my great coat lined with red fox skin, and have bought in the town 12 skins, very good ones, which, when cured, will cost about 12 kr. apiece.

The snow is melting rapidly, and men are about the town with pick-axes, breaking the ice to open up the gutters. We came across a common brown rat dead in the street.

A Whooper Swan was shot in the fiord to-day, and brought into Hansen's shop where it was sold for 5 kr.

Tromsö, April 9th.—Very fine and sunny. We went out in a boat, shooting in the fiord, and got five Long-tailed Ducks, a Queen Eider and another Raven. I felt an awful brute shooting the Raven. It came flopping along the shore when we were lying by it. We also saw a Great Northern Diver, but although we got once within 70 yards, we could not get a shot at it.

The bird stuffer at the Museum is skinning the Eider and Raven for me at 2 kr. each. Two Magpies are nesting in a low tree not 20ft. high in the centre of the town by the church. We saw a Sparrow here to-day. I forgot to mention that the first day we were here, we saw two large light coloured Marsh Tits. The Eiders make a cooing noise very similar to that of the King Eiders. We have now bought everything we want, and are quite ready to start to-morrow. It is quite warm here, only freezing at night, and I only hope the snow won't be too soft crossing the mountains. Grey Crows are absurdly common here, and are very tame. We also saw to-day three Oyster Catchers, which we shot at but missed.

Keniovuopio, April 12th.—We left Tromsö April 10th, at twelve o'clock, with Isak Eriksen, our guide, having had our last cup of coffee with Mr. and Mrs. Hansen and young Hansen; all these three have been very good indeed to us during our visit to the town. We arrived at Skibotten at about one o'clock in the morning. We saw a large shoal of herrings just outside the Lyngen Fiord, and inside a glacier, which looked splendid. I had written to a Finn who lived at Keniovuopio, called Peter Johann, one of two brothers, about two months ago, when I first planned this trip, to be at Skibotten with two sledges and ponies on the 10th of April, and sure enough he met us on the boat. Having landed our luggage, we went to have a hurried sleep at the house of one Rasch. Our guide woke us early on the Sunday morning (11th), and we had some coffee and started with our skins and sledges for Muonioniska, which Johann and his partner promised to do for 90 kr. (just £5), a distance of 203 miles, for the two of us and our guide. We sledged up the river running into the fiord near Skibotten, which was just beginning to thaw, and we were only just in time; a week later and we should have had to have pack ponies, which would have been slower work and considerably more expensive, considering the amount of luggage we are taking.

We passed a Black-bellied Northern Dipper sitting by a bit of open water. The weather was beautiful, the sun very hot and the snow very dazzling, and consequently I broke my snow spectacles in first putting them on. On the way I shot a Rypa and missed another; at about five o'clock we arrived at a hut on the top of the pass, inhabited by an old Finn and his wife, having accomplished 27 miles of our journey, all up hill.

The name of the hut is Helligscoran, and here we put up for the night. With the help of our guide we made some excellent soup from the Rypa, and some Liebig's and vegetable chips, and we also ate some biscuits and sausages. The only thing we could get in the hut was some milk, so we made some coffee and went to bed immediately, about seven o'clock. It was snowing terribly outside and very cold, so we feared a bad to-morrow.

Although the room was very small and there was a good stove, and we kept our clothes on, including boots, we could scarcely sleep for the cold, which must have registered some degrees below zero outside.

We were awake by five o'clock and had some coffee and started. This brings us to to-day. Last night I forgot to mention we tried going on skaes and succeeded beyond our best hopes, being able to get on quite well. The day was again very fine and the sun very hot.

About ten o'clock we arrived at a hut called Silastre, and left the ponies and sledges to water, while Bob and I set out ahead. We arrived at Kilpis-Järvi, a large lake, giving rise to the Muonio river, which is about 15 or 16 miles long, and started walking across. We walked to where there was some open water, evidently a hot spring, and about seven miles from where we started walking, and had a long drink and sat down to wait for the sledges, which arrived about an hour afterwards. We were both very sunburnt, and Bob had the toothache. I washed my handkerchief in the water and put it in the sun to dry, but in about a minute it was frozen stiff like a sheet of paper, and yet we were sitting down, sweating and drinking snow water, which shows how little one feels this dry cold where there is no wind. On leaving the lake and starting down the river, we saw in a small hole a pair of Mallard and put them up. We scraped away the snow on the lake and found it about three feet thick.

We arrived at Peter Johann's house, at about five o'clock, having accomplished about another 25 miles, and made ourselves a similar supper the only difference being he gave us some bread and cream, and we had ham instead of sausage. In the evening Johann's brother brought me in a Hawk Owl which he had shot on the pump just outside the cottage, for which I gave him half a kr., and he seemed very pleased. Our faces burned, so we had to smear them with vaseline.

I bought another fur jacket, as the one I bought in Tromsö was too small for me, and I gave my old one to the guide who was very pleased with it. He does not stand this cold weather half so well as we do, for he coughs and shivers and seems miserable. I only paid 15 kr. for this new jacket which is better and bigger than the Tromsö one, for which I paid double.

Twenty-one wolves were killed here by the natives this winter. They hunt them down on skies when the snow is thick—the wolves can't move fast—and bring them to bay ; then, single-handed, they force one stick into the wolf's mouth, and with another break his back. The foxes are nearly all killed by poison. We saw plenty of tracks of the latter all the way across the mountains, and one or two fresh wolf-tracks.

Naimakka, April 13th.—We rose again early this morning, and I skinned the Hawk Owl, before starting. Judging from the state of her ovaries I don't think she would have laid for at least five weeks. There are no Magpies and Grey Crows to be seen here. The last we saw were at Helligscoran. The sledging was chiefly down the river; there was no sun, and the weather was decidedly cold. The Finns tell me that the large tracks on the mountain snow, were not wolves, but gluttons or Fjeld-fras as they are called.

At a hut, in Vittanyi, a man offered us a white fox in the flesh for 6 kr., but we did not buy it. The Finns say that the river won't be open till the end of May. Peter Johann's brother's name is Mathias, and he is coming on with us as far as Muonioniska. There is also another brother and a sister. The man who lives here, Daniel by name, wants to collect eggs for me. I have asked him to try and get Smew's eggs, but though he knows the bird, he has never yet

A LAPP. *D. M.*

found the egg. He says, he gets 3 kr. 50. for Goshawk's eggs at Kaaresuandro.

Kaaresuandro, April 14th.—We had a long day to-day on the sledge, 42 miles from Sükamopio to here, from eight o'clock to nine. On the way, we saw a herd of about 300 reindeer, searching for moss in the snow. The Lapps were just packing up and making their sledges ready. There were about twelve men that we could see with dogs, preparing to collect the reindeer, and the women and children were packing. On account of the distance we had to go, we had no time to stop and watch them start. A Lapp in a reindeer sledge passed us in the evening.

The reindeer is fastened by a single trace to the underpart of the sledge. The trace passes from between his forelegs, between his hindlegs to the sledge. He is guided by only one rein, which is whipped over from one side to the other, and he keeps up a jogging kind of a trot. They say it is very difficult to sit in one of these sledges and one is easily upset.

At Mannu, one of our stopping places, we each bought a dog for 5 kr.

Firs we first saw about six miles south of Saarenpää. Previously we could see nothing but birch scrub. There was a large stretch of tundra just south of Siekaruopio. Just before reaching Mannu we saw a small flock of Snow Buntings, and Bob shot one.

Muoniovara, April 17th.—We arrived here last night after two days' sledging, which has been most tiring. My eyes have been bunged up too, and I am only too thankful that we have reached our destination at last. There is only one family here, and we have very comfortable quarters. Muonioniska lies on the opposite (Russian) bank of the river, and I suppose there are about ten or twelve families, a church, and a post-office there.

It is thawing here in the middle of the day, and consequently the sledging yesterday was very bad, the horses slipping in sometimes to the tops of their legs. I don't think we left Skibotten a day too early. At Kaarasuandro and at nearly all the houses between there and here, we have seen Magpies; but no Sparrows except here.

There were some Sparrows at Skibotten, but since then these are the first.

This morning we crossed the river to the post-office, and the postmaster showed us some eggs of the Jer Falcon which were taken near 'Niska two years ago, but he wanted 15 kr. for the four. He also says that the Cross Bills are nesting already.

The distance between Skibotten and here is just over 200 miles, and we have done it in six days' sledging. They say we should have taken three weeks instead of one if we had started a week later, on account of the thaw. At one house a woman showed us a female Pine Grosbeak, frozen, which had been shot in January. I met a man called Emil Kumputa, of Hetta, who has promised to collect eggs for me; he has already taken four Goshawk's eggs (14th April). The apparently recognized price for these eggs is 3 kr. each.

We were told to-day that many years ago an Englishman was murdered here, but the natives don't remember either his name or the date. We went for a long walk southwards this evening, and Bob shot a Willow Grouse in pure white plumage; at least I presume it is one, because of its size. They are in winter, however, very similar to Ptarmigan; structurally they do not differ from the British Red Grouse. Professor Newton, in his "Dictionary of Birds" says, they do not occur in the Arctic Regions.

April 18th.—To-day being Easter day we stayed quiet, and didn't go out with guns for fear of shocking the natives. We never found out last Friday was "Good Friday" till yesterday evening, but I am sure we did enough fasting, and had plenty of salt meat. The Roman Catholic law allows one to eat Scoters, which are counted as fish, but I should imagine any one would prefer fish.

There were some Yellow Hammers round the house this morning, but the scarcity of birds strikes one. I went out for a long walk, from five to nine this evening through the pine forests, and never saw one. The spring will come all of a rush, and we are expecting it every moment. It was still thawing to-day, but it freezes every night. The snow is still on an average three feet thick.

The place is infested with fleas, and Bob is quite mad, so much so, that he has made his dog dislike him. My puppy, "Haali" (which means "darling"), is a capital little dog about four months old.

April 19th.—Still thawing. Went for a walk

along the track through the woods, and shot a Siberian Tit. A man called Nilas Geskidalo, of Muonio, called here this morning; he looks an awful blackguard, but says he knows of a Tengmalm's Owl's nest, without eggs. He also says he can get me eggs of "Gala Seski," which I think may mean "Osprey," but I haven't it among my list of Finn bird names. Magpies are quite common here. There is a rather pretty Finnish girl at Muonioniska, who has been in America for three years, and speaks English well; we have made arrangements to stay in her parents' house for two months, with two comfortable rooms, at 30 kr. the two for both rooms. This will be very convenient when Isak our guide goes, as we shall never learn to speak Finnish in the time. Also 50 öre a day each is much cheaper than the living here; of course it does not include food, which we will buy from the house, but we hope to shoot enough birds and catch enough fish to keep us going, when the snow is gone and the river broken up. To-morrow, then, we cross over to the Russian side.

Muonioniska, April 20th.—Isak brought the luggage over the river to-day, and we are settled at last. We went for several walks in the snow, and found some open water both in the big river, between here and Muonionalusta, and in the small stream running into the big river on this side. Bob threw some flies, but caught nothing.

We saw some Grey Crows here, but could not get a shot at them. We unpacked in the evening. We had brought two boxes dried figs, two jars dried plums, two pots of Liebig, two tins Brands' essence, four boxes of golf biscuits, six pots of jam, marmalade and chocolate. We can always get fresh milk, coffee, butter, black rye bread, and a sort of biscuit in the town here.

April 21st.—I shot three Siberian Tits to-day. I saw no other sort of bird the whole day. It was freezing in the shade the whole day, and last night we had a very sharp frost.

April 22nd.—There was a very sharp frost last night, and we were able to walk about on the snow during the whole day. Bob was on skaes. I got some letters from home to day, and also the *Weekly Times*; so we heard that Oxford had won the sports and the boat race.

Nilas brought in a nest of Siberian Jays (three eggs) almost fresh, which he had taken at Muoniosara. I gave him a kr. for them, and he rushed out of the room apparently to get a drink. I skinned a Siberian Tit in the morning, and blew the eggs, and started out for a long stroll, but never a bird did I see or hear. It seems astonishing that there should not be more, but I was out from eleven to seven.

There were a lot of loose reindeer grazing about in the forest, and, ungainly as they are, they looked very picturesque on the snow among the firs.

Bob came home more successful, having found a nest of Cross Bills just hatching. The four embryos I put in spirit, and two of the eggs which had only cracked I have kept. They are very similar to those of the Greenfinch. He also saw some more Siberian Tits, and a Northern Black-bellied Dipper. The nests of the Jay and the Cross Bill I have described elsewhere.

April 23rd.—Went out to the east of the village. In a hollow about seven miles from the town, I saw just in front of me a fine Cross Bill cross the track. I walked after it into the wood, and just as I got within shot, I heard a "mobbing" going on ahead, so I spared the Cross Bill, and went for the "mobbing," supposing there might be an Owl, and sure enough there was a Hawk Owl sitting on the top of a very high fir tree, being "mobbed" by Siberian Jays. The Owl didn't seem the slightest bit afraid of me, so I sat down and ate my lunch which consisted of some chocolate and biscuits. I counted at least ten Jays, and after I had sat there and watched these birds for about a quarter of an hour, I put up my gun and fired at the Owl. I saw the bird distinctly drop, but could not see for the thickness of the wood whether it touched the ground. I, however, did not go up to it directly, but waited to get a shot at the Jays, but they carefully kept out of range. But imagine my disgust at finding no Owl on the ground. The air here is so clear, and the tree was so high, it must have been out of shot, and since I had only No. 8 shot with me, the only consolation was that the bird was probably uninjured. I only heard it give one screech as it sat on the tree. A little further on, I saw a Grey-headed Yellow Wagtail by an open piece of water in a small mountain torrent—but I could not get a good shot at it.

Bob found another Cross Bill's nest on the 'rara side of the river, and shot the bird, which I have skinned this evening. He broke one of the three fresh eggs; the bird contained one egg nearly ready for laying.

An Englishman, named John Gow, was here about five years ago, as far as I can gather from the natives. They thought he was mad, because he bought anything they chose to bring him, fleas and bugs and anything, and he paid high prices too.

Woolley they all know of, and some of them remember him; he had been in the house we live in now. These, they say, are the only foreigners of any nation who have been here before us. The man who was murdered was apparently coming here, but never actually arrived. The natives seem very religious; we can hear prayers going on in the next room at all times of the day. They are also, as a rule, remarkably honest; all the houses are left open both day and night.

I bought a pair of skaes to-day for 5 kr., and two sticks that were thrown in, and had an hour's practice this evening, preparatory to go far to-morrow. The snow is getting so soft in the middle of the days, that one cannot get about without them. None of the migrants have arrived yet, unless such birds as the Yellow Hammer and Dipper arrived before us. There is a saying in Lapland that "when the Brambling arrives, the Grayling come out of the deep holes."

April 24th.—Got up this morning at five o'clock, and at 5.30 had an enormous breakfast of boiled potatoes and pancakes, bread and butter, and marmalade, and started out on skaes at six to the north-east of the village. We had to start early, as the sun by mid-day thaws the crust on the snow, and one cannot get about, anyhow, in the afternoon.

We made for the wood where yesterday I saw a Hawk Owl, and after a few minutes I saw what I took to be a Pine Cross Bill get up some way in front of me, and made for him. It however flew some distance, but in a few minutes I heard him singing (I knew the song from one we had alive in our rooms at Harrow) about one hundred yards off, and at the same moment I heard a shot, and shouted to Bob to ask what he had got. He said, a "Cross Bill," at which I felt much relieved, and went up to him, when, to my surprise, I found he had killed a Grosbeak. Within a few hundred yards I shot a cock Cross Bill, and a little later on I found a pair of Siberian Jays, which we killed, I the male and Bob the female. After I had killed the male, the female sat up at the top of a high tree, and gave us the most delightful song, which I waited to hear, till I told Bob of her whereabouts. In the evening one of the boys here brought me a nest of Jays (four eggs), taken this side of the river. We got home about two, and went out again without skaes till seven, but I saw nothing.

D. M.

PEREGRINE FALCON IN SNOW-STORM.

Sunday, April 25th.—On skinning the Pine Grosbeak, which was a green bird tinged with golden yellow and some mauve on the feathers round the gape, I found, to my astonishment, that it was a male bird.

We went to church to-day. The church is a large wooden building on the highest ground in the town, and can be seen some distance away. The whole service, which is in Finnish, was performed by a lusty parson, who screamed enough to deafen most people, but fortunately he was occasionally checked by a doleful hymn, which would have done admirably for Good Friday instead of the first Sunday after Easter, as to-day is. The women, as in the Roman church, sat on the left side, with handkerchiefs and towels tied about their heads, and the men sat opposite. Though the church is enormous for the village—I suppose it would hold 1,000 people—there were only 17 women and 33 men present, most of whom were boys comprising the choir, but they did not, as far as we could hear, sing; but it is not astonishing we didn't hear them, considering the loudness of the voice of the postmaster, who accompanies on a bad harmonium. At moments, when the postmaster could not reach the high notes, there seemed to be quite a slump in the noises.

At the end of the service, the parson, according to Isak, gave out that there was going to be a funeral on Tuesday, and on Wednesday at ten o'clock there would be some cows sold, and since he was acting as auctioneer, gratis, he would, if no one objected, pocket the collection himself.

Of course all eyes were turned on us during the service, and Isak says, that our coming here is quite the event of the year, and will be talked about for many years to come.

At Tromsö, where we were the first "tourists" as they called us, the local newspaper got hold somehow of our names, and in a paragraph concerning us gave full descriptions of our journey, concluding by saying that we had come here to fish, and with that object had taken the fishing and also the shooting of the Muonio river and valley. The fishing I suppose would be some 500 miles in extent, not counting small rivers, and the shooting some 10,000 square miles. I wonder what they thought we had paid for it. It also said "with a view to buying it" and yet they put us up at the principal hotel for 6 kr. a day. They would be astonished to hear that we are living here at 1 kr. a day.

April 26th.—To-day we were up at 2.20 a.m. and out by 3.30. Bob going to the 'rara side, and I stopping this side. When I had got about three miles from the town, I heard what I took to be the note of a Brown Owl, within two or three hundred yards of me, on the further side of a small valley; but it could not on second thoughts be a Brown Owl; they do not occur so far north; so I immediately made for where I thought the bird was. When I arrived there after much trouble, I saw nothing, and waited to listen, when I heard it again further on. I naturally thought the bird had flown on in front of me, so I followed again, and again the same thing happened, and again, and again. The note was louder each move I made, and appeared to me slightly different to an Owl's note, yet I couldn't imagine what else it might be. I continued for about three miles tracing this note, stopping every few hundred yards and listening, picturing to myself Eagles Owls, Lapp Owls, Ural Owls, and all the big Owls I could think of, till at last I came to a huge swamp frozen over all but a small piece of open water in the centre, and by this I sat down and wept, for I was streaming with perspiration, and the sound had stopped. As soon as I got cool, I started to return, when a tremendous boom came from the open water, by which I saw a real live Crane standing, and throwing back his head and screaming as hard as he could. Often have I heard these birds at the Zoo, but never during that hour had it occurred to me it might be a Crane. If any-one has seen the sternum of a Crane, he might well expect the owner to make such a noise. Of course it was impossible to get within shot, so I in turn gave a tremendous scream, which sent the huge bird soaring over the opposite fell.

Coming back I obtained a hen Cross Bill. I got home about eleven, and Bob returned about 12.30 having got a Three-toed Wood-pecker, a pair of Grosbeaks, and a Siberian Jay. He had seen a Goshawk, and a Hawk Owl, also a pair of Willow Grouse.

The name of the owner of this house is Karl Latti (Latti is the name of the house). The people here are known by the names of either their houses or villages.

April 27th.—A boy brought us to-day two Eagle Owl's eggs taken about twelve miles off, and three Siberian Jay's eggs, for which I gave him 5 kr.

We skinned the birds this morning. To-day came the bills for the week, apart from the rent of the two rooms (50 öre a day each), the

D. M.

SEA EAGLE.

food came to, in all, 16 kr.; but we have been very extravagant in the way of flour and milk, and plenty of flour and potatoes bought last week will serve us this week.

I find one can buy quite decent Russian cigarettes in the town at 1 kr. 10 a hundred. The cigars which are made in Jacobsmad cost three a penny, but are not good. I foolishly brought only two pipes and have broken one. Anyone coming to an out-of-the-way place should, I'm sure, bring up plenty of pipes, as any he does not use would make capital presents for the men, and would even do in exchange for eggs, etc.

To-day is our first cloudy day, but still it is thawing now (1 p.m.) and we are going out to-night at eight to stop the night in the woods.

April 28th.—We left the village last night at six o'clock, and walked up the river in the slush on the top of the ice for about five miles, which took us nearly three hours. The snow on the ice is thawed into slush with a crust on the top, and nothing is more tiring than this kind of walking, at every step expecting to drop a foot through the crust. We then left the river and walked into the forest about 1½ miles, where dripping wet, we lit a fire, and made ourselves warm and tried to get dry. By 9.30 the sun had set, but it was not really dark the whole night. There must have been at least 10° of frost. However, we had a good fire, and had brought a mackintosh rug to sit on, and on this we sat with my dog Haali, looking at the fire, and talking of what we should do on the morrow. I had expected to hear and see some Owls during the night, but we saw none, though I was awake the whole night. The only sound we heard was the call of the cock Rypa, which might be heard on all sides in this lonely forest. The call is very similar to that of the British Grouse.

Before the sun rose, I went for a little stroll, and put up a hen Capercailzie from her bough on a bare pine and at sunrise we had breakfast consisting of three dried figs, two sticks of chocolate and some bread; also some brandy and water, for which we were very thankful, as it was, in spite of a good fire, very cold. Next time we camp out, we will each take a mackintosh rug and roll ourselves up and go to sleep. The sun rose at about 2.30, and after breakfast we started west, to find a place where Bob, the day before, had seen a Goshawk. This, however, we failed to find. One has no idea how easy it is to get lost in these forests, for to-day if it had not been for meeting a Lapp on a reindeer sledge, we should have gone in the opposite direction to 'Niska, when we intended to return.

We first of all came upon a large frozen lake, and walking across this, reached the opposite side, where we put down our fishing baskets and separated for a time. I came across an Osprey's nest by the side of the lake, and round it were flying a pair of Ravens. It was too early for the Ospreys, so I did not climb the tree, although I suspected the Ravens had eggs; another reason was that I was too tired. The only bird I got was a Siberian Tit, a very fine specimen. Bob returned to the rendezvous with two grey squirrels, very pretty creatures, which we skinned on the spot, because my dog required food. We could hear some Cranes calling in the far distance—there seemed to be several all round.

After resting on the shore of the lake for some time, we returned, passing on the way home a pair of Rypa, the cock bird of which was already assuming the summer plumage, being reddish on the head and neck. The natives say these birds will be laying in a week. Although the Russian law imposes a fine of 16 kr. on any bird killed out of season, there is apparently no law about eggs, which are eaten by the natives.

The fine for killing a Rypa in Norway is 6 kr., in Sweden 10 kr.

We returned about twelve, and were very thankful to get a cup of coffee and some bread which we found prepared for us. This evening, I am going out with a man who has seen some Woodpeckers, and so intend to sleep from now till six.

April 29th.—I only managed to get four hours sleep yesterday, as Isak kept walking about the room and I could not get him out. After a meal of pancakes and potatoes at 5.30, I started out with a guide to the eastward of the town. He showed me the nest of a Tengmalm's Owl, which is apparently ready for eggs; we also saw two Goshawks and a Hawk Owl. I found a Jay's nest with three eggs and shot the old bird as she came from the nest, and in the night I shot a Rypa. I got back this morning about one o'clock, thoroughly tired, after a walk of about twenty miles at a break-neck pace through slush, alternating on occasions with snow with a nerve-shaking crust, and water two feet deep.

April 30th.—There has been a good thaw the last few days, and Redpoles are coming in fast, and to-day I saw the first Fieldfare. First the melting of the snow lays bare the seeds and berries; then come the seed-eaters then the bird-eaters in the form of Rough-legged Buzzards, which I saw to-day—Bob also saw some. I shot a Siberian Tit and a squirrel to-day, and saw a Merlin, and some Golden Eye Ducks. Bob shot a beautiful male Golden Eye this morning, and got up to within 200 yards of Cranes. He says he saw another sort of a duck, but is not certain of what species—probably a Tufted Duck.

Bob shot his dog to-day, and I'm not sorry for it, for a more disobedient little cur I never saw.

Isak, our guide and philosopher, left to-day. He wants to be back in Tromsö by the 17th of May, but I doubt if he'll manage it, as the river is most dangerous for sledging—at least as far south as this. He has been most useful to us, and I'm very sorry to part with him, as we were the best of friends.

May 1st.—Bob and I went up the bank of the river to try and get some duck. I had four long shots at Golden Eye and got one fine old male. We saw about a dozen Geese, which, though not appearing very wild, would not let us get within shot. We also saw some Pintails.

Sunday, May 2nd.—We did nothing to-day, but skin the birds we had previously shot. The snow is gone now from the most exposed parts, but the ice, except in the rapids and a few other places, remains pretty thick.

May 3rd.—I went up to the top of the fell behind 'Niska to-day, which was a pretty good toil. I got a pair of Jays, and a beautiful grey squirrel. I found a large Hawk's nest, and a Rough-legged Buzzard was flying about it within shot, but I spared her for the eggs.

Bob shot a Redwing, and another fine male Golden Eye, and saw a Snipe arrive, chased by a Merlin. I saw a pair of Pipits on the swamp behind the town, but could not say for certain whether they were "red-throated," or "meadow."

We went and sat on the rocks by the rapids this evening, and a finer sight could not be imagined—this huge river, 400 to 500 yards across, rushing down between fir forests, and with great blocks of ice being tossed about like small pieces of wood; and to add to the charm of it a glorious sunset of gold and green, and Pintail Ducks, and Golden Eyes, whisking up the centre in pairs and small flocks.

May 4th.—Last night Nilas brought in a Jay on her three eggs, nest and all. It seemed a pity to kill her, but as I could not hope to get a perfect skeleton otherwise, I determined to transform her into one. The three eggs are very fine ones, all different, one of them with large mauve blotches.

From the top of the fell, yesterday, I got a wonderful view of this part of Lapland covered with fir forest, all except the snow-capped fells around, most of them much higher than the one on which I was standing. The slender twigs of the birch against the dark green pines give a mauve appearance, and this accounts for the mauve belts one sees in the distance in the forests.

To-day is a wet day and consequently there is a slump in noteworthy facts. Nilas told me last night he knew of a Woodpecker's nest with one egg, and we are going to visit it on Saturday next.

The common bird in these forests, the Siberian Jay, *Perisoreus infaustus* (Linn.), is one of the most amusing birds in the world—tamer no bird could be, for wherever one walks this bird accompanies. Its notes are most varied, from a song as good as any Thrush's to a scream resembling that of our British Jay. The dead bird, or a stuffed bird in a museum, looks a more or less sombre coloured bird; but a gleam of sunshine on its tail through the pine trees makes it even brighter than the russet tail of the Redstart.

By looking through the telescope this evening, I could see on the water in front of this house, Widgeon, Tufted, and Golden Eye. The Golden Eyes in courting the females were going through all manner of grotesque attitudes, and particularly that well-known one of throwing their heads over their backs. All the ducks are in particularly beautiful plumage.

Coming back from my walk this evening, I put up a pair of Moor Hens near the town. Bob saw a Black-throated Diver, and some Reed Buntings.

May 5th.—To-day has been a fine windy day, and a most curious thing has happened. At a certain time in the middle of the day, there appears to have been a regular hurricane on the river for a few minutes. I was in the woods and consequently did not feel it much. But when I returned, we walked down to the rapid, and found the ice piled up on the bank—huge blocks twelve feet square, and two or three feet high, piled up one on the top of another, in some places eight or nine feet high. It seems almost impossible that such a thing could have happened, and whether these blocks were raised by pressure from below, or heaved up bodily by some huge waves, I cannot say. But the whole scene presented the most curious appearance, and

THE MUONIO RIVER.

to see some of these huge masses of ice,come rushing down the rapid with the sun setting behind, and giving the most beautiful light effects, was a sight one will never forget. What the river can be like at Tornea, I cannot imagine, for there are many rivers as large as this running into it, and this is 400 or 500 yards across at the rapids.

I shot to-day two Redwings in beautiful plumage, a Siberian Tit and a gorgeous cock Rypa. Rypas seem to be very common here, as I find plenty of droppings, but unless one has a good dog, one sees very few. This bird has finished the moult of his head, the feathers of which seem similar to those of the English *lagopus scoticus*, except for the white patches round the bill and eye. The feathers which can be detected under the white ones on the back will, I suppose, appear in a week or two.

Bob shot a male Pintail, and came back with an adventurous boat story.

May 6th.—I got a clutch of six Magpie's eggs to-day, probably the first clutch of Magpie's ever taken here, as I doubt whether the birds have been here long.

Bob shot a Reed Bunting in perfect plumage and also a fine pair of Tufted Duck. The male bird makes a croak very similar to that of a Crow.

In walking through these forests one comes across large ant heaps, inhabited by large ants. I opened one to-day and found within a large supply of resin in small lumps about the size of peas, from the fir trees.

The contents of the gizzards of four Siberian Jays which I have examined, contain the remains of the bleaberry (*vaccinium myrtillus*) and nothing else. This seems to be the food of many birds here, the Grosbeak and Willow Grouse for instance. The mauve round the bill of the Grosbeak is no doubt merely the stain from the juice of these berries. We came across five Skylarks this evening.

May 7th.—A boy brought in four Sparrows' eggs this evening; I don't suppose there are Sparrows' eggs from the Arctic Circle in many collections.

We had pike for breakfast, and Pintail soup and Rypa for dinner to-day. The last two or three days we have had nothing but Golden Eye soup. I also got hold of a fork to-day, and was able to eat fairly decently.

The crop and gizzard of the Rypa I skinned this morning was full of bleaberries.

I shot to-day another cock Rypa in half moult, with a few white feathers still on the neck, also a cock Reed Bunting. There are plenty of these latter birds about now, but they are all, as far as I can see, cock birds.

I've never seen anybody work so hard as the people do here. The girl has to milk the cows, call us, give us our meals, make our beds, scrub all the floors, bake the bread, wash the clothes, fetch the water, in fact, almost everything. The men are cutting wood the whole day, wet or fine. There is a shoemaker staying in the house, who has made us each a pair of slippers (4 kr.), and a pair of top-boots, water-tight, and reaching about six inches above the knee (13 kr.) They are both capital, and I am sure we'll wear nothing else during our stay here.

The whole surface of the main stream is now covered with broken ice. I daresay the gale that has been blowing these last few days has had much to do with breaking up the ice.

May 8th.—We saw three new birds to-day; Bob saw a Greenshank and obtained it; he also shot a Teal. I saw a House Martin and a Brambling—the latter I obtained.

The crops and gizzards of two Reed Buntings, which I skinned this morning, contained nothing but bleaberries. In fact most of the birds appear to feed on these. They are, of course, last autumn's berries which have been frozen up in the snow. I saw to-day for the first time some frog-spawn in the marshes. There are plenty of insects about now—river flies, some small moths, and two different brown butterflies.

With the showers of the last few days the snow appears to be almost entirely gone except on the fells, and these are covered only on the north side and in the gullies. Less ice is coming down the river. Bob tried spinning in the small stream near the town, but caught nothing. We had Tufted Duck soup to-night for dinner, and excellent it was; to-morrow, Teal and Rypa.

Old Nilas is sick or drunk, and did not appear to-day.

May 10th. — Yesterday, being Sunday, we spent a lazy day, but instead of going to bed I started out northwards about eleven o'clock, just after sunset, and got about five miles into the forest by sunrise, which was about a quarter to one o'clock, and for the first time since we have been here, the woods seemed alive with birds. Almost before sunrise, I could hear the pleasant song of the Redwing from all parts of the wood, and during the day I came across many of last year's nests of these birds. I shot one, a Brambling, and a pretty pair of Mealy Redpoles. The note of the Brambling is similar to that of the Chaffinch, only more harsh.

Many Fieldfares were flying about, but they seemed very wild and shy.

I also shot a female Widgeon, and a pair of Rypa. First I shot the female as she rose, and the male, as soon as she dropped, dropped likewise and seemed apparently wounded—fluttering about on the ground and jumping up into the air—but on going up to where my hand was only within a foot of him, he rose, and flew gaily away, but not very far, so I got him afterwards. He was further advanced in the moult than any I had previously shot, for not only were his head and neck fully moulted, but some new feathers were showing on his back and above his tail. The female also has many new feathers on her neck.

On returning, I saw a mountain hare, and followed in pursuit; but the brute would keep out of gun shot, and merely went round in a circle stopping every now and then to look at me. It was while following her that I saw a bird I had least expected to see up here, viz., a Barn Owl (*strix flammea*); I got within five yards of it sitting on the ground, when it flew a little distance and again pitched on the ground. It looked most out of place in a fir forest.

The Yellow Hammer seems to alter its note throughout the whole night.

I saw several Greenshanks and several small Sandpipers on the river this morning. This is the first day I have noticed any diminution of the flood. The river has dropped six inches during the night.

The Ducks were swarming on the river early this morning, and I had a good opportunity of seeing some of the rarer ones. The Tufted Duck seems to make a croak very similar to that of a Crow. The Widgeon make, besides their well-known whistle, a scolding noise. It is very hard to put the notes of any birds, especially Duck, into so many words.

I got a clutch of Magpies (six) and Grey Crows (four) to-day. Also a male Hawk Owl and a nest of six eggs, two of which contained embryos of about two days.

The girl tells me this is a very early year, for last year the snow and ice had not even begun to go by the end of May. There is a thunder-storm this evening. Wheelwright only mentions hearing thunder once at Quickiock.

May 11th. — The postmaster tells me he has been unable to get me the Jer Falcon's eggs this year because it is early. The ones that were taken two years ago were taken at Enontekio. He tells me of a man who has taken four Passerine Owl's eggs, and I intend to buy them, although he wants 10 kr. each. The post-master has also some Eagle Owl's eggs.

To-day I spent in skinning and making a skeleton of the Hawk Owl. I bought to-day some eggs which a boy had taken last year, including three Osprey's and eight Rough-legged Buzzard's, for which I gave him 10 kr.

May 12th.—Nothing of very much interest to-day. The only new arrivals are Ruff and Whinchat. Karl Laati told me that some years ago he took a clutch of Passerine Owl's eggs and sold them.

Bob spent most of the day in trolling in the bay for trout and pike, and had a trout on for two minutes, but lost it. This shows, however, it isn't too early to start fishing. These last few days have been the hottest we have had, very cloudy and muggy.

May 13th.—On sexing a Greenshank this morning I found in the œsophagus a pike over three inches long. It also contained a ripe egg.

As far as I can make out, there are five species of birds found from here to Alaska and nowhere else—namely, *Surnia funerea, Strix lapponica, Cyanecula suecica, Phylloscopus borealis,* and *Archibuteo lagopus,* and perhaps *Anthus cervinus*, though whether this latter occurs in Alaska I am not certain. This would go much in favour of considering the Palæarctic and Nearctic regions equal to one in reality, which has been termed by Professor Newton "Holarctic." But possibly only Alaska need be added to the Palæarctic region.

The clavicles of the Hawk Owl do not unite to form a furcula, but are only joined to the keel of the sternum by a strong ligament. The Barn Owl is apparently alone in having a complete merry thought.

May 14th.—I left Muonioniska to-day in a North-easterly direction, with a Finn staying in the house, as guide. We went in search of "Houkka," *i.e.* Hawks and Owls, and he carried my bag which contained white bread and butter and his own food, while I took my fishing basket almost full of cartridges and skinning and blowing apparatus, and I think, with the gun and a heavy hatchet, I carried much the heavier weight. Our first day's journey was all through the forest. The whole way we were accompanied by Siberian Jays, and saw very little else. We came across a fresh dead reindeer calf.

At about eight or nine in the evening, after reaching Sieppigärvi, which is 26 miles as the crow flies from Muonioniska, we found we were stopped by a small river coming out of the lake, which was in flood; but our first night's resting place was near, so the Finn shouted at the top of his voice for a boat, and, on none appearing, I fired two shots across the lake. Still there came no answer. The Finn then proceeded to light a fire and make ready to sleep in the wood, while I watched two Ospreys fishing in the lake, calling out to each other occasionally, and they evidently had a nest close by. After about an hour, finding the place very damp, and having nothing to lie on, I determined to try again for a boat, and so fired several shots and shouted as loud as I could. To my delight, at last one came round the corner, rowed by a very pretty little girl about fourteen years old.

Within half-an-hour, we were at the house Sieppi, and got some milk, and they cooked some excellent pike for me, after which I started to write this. As I write, there are six children ushered into the room to stare at me, for this is the first, and may be the last time they will see an Englishman; the woman is describing to them my good points. They particularly fancy my beard, which is thicker than any man's up here—nobody seems to grow more than down.

May 15th.—Last night I bought a sort of cheese, which being very indigestible, I thought would do well, since a little would go a long way. We hired a boat from the house, and had the most delightful row across the lake and up a small stream for about five miles to Gerasjärvi. I saw all manner of birds, Ducks of all sorts, wild Geese, Dusky Redshanks, Greenshanks, Ruffs, Sandpipers, Stints, and Whimbrels. The day was very hot, and even an old Raven that flew down the stream about ten feet over my head was panting for breath with his mouth wide open. A pair of Arctic Terns flew over me in the lake and also a pair of Ospreys, and I shot one of the former. I also shot a pair of Willow Grouse, coming full swing down the stream, which delighted the natives, for they had evidently never seen a bird shot flying, and they made me undo my gun, and show them all its parts. I also went up to a box put for Golden Eyes, and found two eggs.

I could not help thinking that if I only bring back some empty shells of carbonate of lime, this craze for bird's eggs has brought me into contact with some of the most interesting birds at their most interesting time.

On landing the further side of Gerasjärvi, we had a most tedious walk up the mountain, and saw absolutely no birds but Whimbrels, Bramblings, and Redwings. Down the other side into the valley of the Ounasjoki, a walk of about fifteen miles brought us in the evening to the river itself. We saw a pair of Goosanders on a small lake on the way, and I shot a dark coloured squirrel (orava).

I got some coffee and milk at a small house here to-night, and I saw also a nice bed of hay. The old man showed me a miscellaneous collection of eggs, containing some of the common English Thrush eggs, which he considered very rare and wanted me to buy, and he also had a mummified young Black Woodpecker, which he got in the forest behind the house.

The river is not so big as the Muonio, but is apparently full of pike, as I saw plenty of small ones all along the bank.

May 16th.—This morning my Finn guide did not appear, and I thought probably he was unwell, but a Lapp who had arrived during the night indicated that he knew of some nests, by repeating several birds' names, and so I started off with him in a boat up the river, leaving the Finn behind and my bag containing the food, intending to return at night. We went up close to the bank, he rowing and I steering, and both of us punting at the rapids for about five miles, when we came to a broadening of the river with many small islands. On one of these, about three yards from the waters' edge, I took a pair of Black-throated Diver's eggs, and on another about two yards from the edge, a pair of Red-throated Diver's eggs; there being in neither case a nest, only a flat place made on the grass, and a flat run down to the waters' edge.

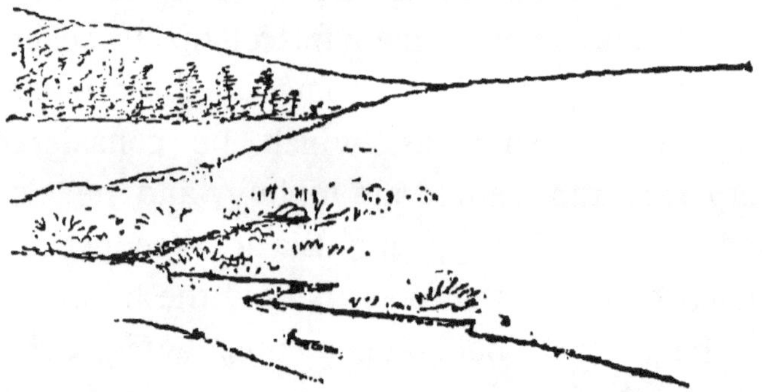

On neither occasion could I catch a glimpse of the birds. There were several pairs of Golden Eyes up the river, and I also saw, for the first time, a pair of Red-breasted Mergansers. We then landed, and trudged up the most awful hill I've ever come across; on the further side we entered a ravine with rocks sometimes fifty or sixty feet high on either side, and at the bottom a small brook swarming with Dippers. The low ground was covered with and birch, in and out flew Camberwell beauties, and a small bright coloured brownish butterfly, the upper wings uniform brown, the lower ones orange spotted with dark brown. At last, after about two miles of ravine, we came to a Hawk's nest in the cliff about twenty feet above the brook. The ground underneath was covered with Rypa bones, chiefly the pelvis and humerus. The Lapp cut some birch trees and laid them up the cliff, and I sat below, hoping to have in a few minutes some Jer Falcon's eggs in my hands, for although we had not seen the birds (I thought probably our scrambling up the ravine had frightened them) it was evidently a fresh nest. Up he clambered, but to my disappointment there were no eggs, so I made a sketch of the nest, and we walked away.

He called the bird "Tunturi koppello haukka," which I think means Jer Falcon.

After a little way I lost my bearings completely, and had absolutely no idea where we were; and after six or seven hours' hard walking I determined to sit down and eat something, having had nothing all day but some milk when I started, and now the sun was low and it must have been ten or eleven o'clock. It was during this meal that I made a mistake, for, having finished eating the only bit of bread in my fishing basket, I took a drop of whisky

from my flask, and the poor old Lapp looked so lovingly at it, that I thought I must give him some, so I handed him the flask, while I lit my pipe; but before my pipe was half alight,

LAPP HUT.

he had finished the lot and the flask was nearly full to start with.

In vain after this did I repeat my stock sentence to him " Mie dahun gotia " (I want to go home); he went on jabbering and talking to himself, and would not listen to any words of mine, so I thought we would have to spend the night where we were, and I had absolutely no idea where that was ; but soon he got up, and leading the way, half holding on to the trees and half balancing himself with his gun, we started on again, and within a couple of hours reached the river, but not where we had left it. On the further side of it was a Lapp encampment with some reindeer, and an old Lapp woman rowed across and fetched us. We walked into the hut, a wooden square one, and very dark inside ; within were two girls, and some children, and in the centre a huge fire filling the hut with smoke.

The first thing I did was to ask for some milk, but they did not move, so I presumed they did not understand me, or had none, so I sat down and lit my pipe and waited to see if they would give me anything. At last the old woman fetched a tin from a shelf and began grinding some coffee, and fearing perhaps I should get none, as soon as she had ground sufficient I rushed for it, and securing a pot made some on the fire for myself. I searched every corner in the room for milk but could not find any. Meanwhile the old man had gone to sleep on the floor, and the girls and the children turned into some hay in the corner, for it must have been about midnight. After the coffee I walked out, and here I am sitting by the side of the river writing this by the light of the rising sun, and not knowing where I am, or where I am going to-morrow.

May 17th.—When I returned to the hut last night I found the old woman had made a most comfortable bed for me, in a corner of the room, of hay covered with reindeer skins, so I took off my coat and boots and left her sitting by the fire smoking a huge pipe, and wasn't long in getting to sleep.

I woke up this morning, I suppose close on mid-day, and found some coffee and milk waiting for me which the girls had prepared, and I gave them each a cigarette which they very much enjoyed.

After this, I tried to make up my mind what to do, for it was raining hard and I did not much fancy trying to find my way back to 'Niska, which might have been fifty or sixty miles off for all I knew.

But, fortunately for me, the Finn appeared with my bag. I don't know if he intended all the time not to stop here, and to catch me up, or whether he had been ill, or what; but he certainly did well in not sleeping here, for I was itching all over this morning, and had to wash in the icy cold water of the river.

About 2.20 we started out in the rain, I carrying the bag and my gun, and he taking the fishing basket. We walked over a lot of barren ground, and in the evening arrived at a cottage where we got some coffee, and the men took me to a Rough-legged Buzzard's nest, not half a mile away from the house, in a rock very similar to the Falcon's nest yesterday, and from it I took four almost white eggs, one slightly incubated. We went another five miles or so, and reached Peltorourma ; there, in a house quite palatial compared to the hut this morning, I had a grand meal of pike, bread and butter, and milk, and took off my dripping clothes.

There is a man staying here dressed like a commercial traveller in a brown bowler, who has with him a collection of Finnish literature, and from him I bought at sixpence a phrase book of English and Finnish, which I hope will prove very useful.

May 18th.—To-day we started on our return journey, and had a very long day of it. Starting at six o'clock from Peltorourma, together with a Lapp who knew of an Eagle's nest, we went up a hill behind the house, and there was the nest in a crevice in a rock some thirty feet from the ground. I scrambled up, and, to my great disappointment, found it empty, since, after seeing two Golden Eagles soaring over-head, I had naturally expected to find either young ones or eggs.

But on coming away, another Lapp brought me two eggs, which he had taken in April from this very nest, and I had to pay 10 kr. each for them, although they were unblown, perfectly rotten of course, and probably never could have been blown.

Thence we made for the river Ormasjoki, some 25 miles from Peltorourma, and we arrived there about mid-day, having beaten several swamps, and taken nests of Pintail, Golden Eye, and wild Goose (I'm not quite certain which the large Goose here is, bean or grey-leg), and five Redwings' nests.

At a Lapp's hut by the side of the river, we made ourselves some coffee, and, crossing the river, we ascended Aulastunturi (2124 feet). Half way up I took two Rough-legged Buzzard's eggs, and two more—very small ones—close to the summit.

This evening, or rather early in the morning of the 19th, we arrived at Sieppiajarvi, where a boy brought me a pair of Black-throated Diver's eggs he had taken.

Many of the mountain lakes were still frozen over; some even we walked across. We had seventeen hours walking to-day, and I suppose covered very nearly 50 miles.

May 19th.—I arrived home to-day, and was very pleased to see Bob. He had taken an Osprey's nest some eight or nine miles from the town and shot the old bird.

May 20th.–To-day was spent in keeping quiet, and comparing notes, and writing diaries out.

May 21st.–I took my first Tengmalm's Owl's eggs to-day, and also a clutch of Snipe's eggs.

It seems curious that the men here should cut down so many trees, and leave them where they are cut; for the whole place is strewn with rotting trees lying on the ground, and makes walking about most difficult. It is a curious fact that pine and fir trees when they rot while standing, warp from right to left, and birch from left to right. This is almost invariably the case. I wonder if anybody has noticed this, and can account for it.

May 22nd.—We took a clutch of five Reed Buntings to-day, and four Grey Crow's eggs. The river has been very high, and is now sinking fast.

May 24th.—Neither the nest of the Fieldfare or Redwing differs, as far as I can see, from that of the Blackbird. A clutch of four Rough-legged Buzzards, which I took yesterday, prove something, namely, that brighter coloured eggs are laid first; for two with bright marks were a bit set, and the other two plain ones quite fresh; but I believe this is not always the case.

When out to-day I noticed a Whimbrel alight on the very top of a dead pine, and I shot a fine pair to-day. I have made the Tengmalm's Owl into a skeleton, as she was scarcely worth preserving. It is snowing like anything this evening. Post to-morrow.

May 26th.—To-day is quite a warm day, and there are plenty of House Martins about. The House Martin I saw on the 10th was evidently a mistaken bird, who came too early. I also shot a Willow Wren. I got some eggs of the Siberian Tit to-day, and spent all day in blowing and skinning.

May 27th.—I got some beautiful Kestrel's eggs to-day, and a clutch of seven Magpie's. To-day was quite hot, and there are plenty of

Wheat Ears about. Bob shot a Ruff, with an almost white head and ruff. He says the flies in the woods are very numerous to-day. To-morrow we go woodpeckering.

May 28th.—To-day we went to Sirkojärvi, some 12 miles away from 'Niska, and saw on the way a Great Black Woodpecker, to which we were first attracted by a low "boo," like the first syllable of a Wood Owl's note. We followed it some way, and saw it hewing chunks of wood six inches long out of trees. The only other note it made, was similar to the single call of the Kestrel.

In the evening we went to the nest where Bob shot the Osprey, and took the three eggs. I got a clutch of Middle-spotted Woodpecker's eggs, and two clutches of Capercailzie's. We slept at the Finn's house on the lake.

May 29th.—We returned home, starting at five o'clock in the morning, and reached here at two, when we had a good meal. We saw the great Black Woodpecker on the way back. During the afternoon Bob caught six grayling, and all within half an hour. They seem to lie at present in the rapids just above any piece of rough water. The men caught some trout in the nets here for the first time.

In the evening a man told us he knew of a Short-eared Owl's nest, so we went and took it, about 3 or 4 miles up the river on a dry piece of ground surrounded by swamps, and with small bushes covering the ground. In a small hollow under one of these bushes, lined with dry grass and some of its own larger feathers, were five incubated eggs. We waited some time to get a shot at the old birds, but they were much too shy.

On the way we shot a pair of Widgeon, and a beautiful Blackcock sitting upon one of the hay sheds by the river. I had no idea the Short-eared Owl would perch on trees; but several times the bird perched on top of a high fir tree to see where we were.

Of the two clutches of Capercailzie's eggs I got, one set is much the larger, and the natives tell me that the old birds lay the larger eggs, and the small eggs are laid by birds of the previous year.

The Blackcock appears to be rare here. They tell me they seldom find the eggs. I see that Wheelwright excludes it from his Quickiock list.

May 30th.—Clutch of twelve Tufted Duck. Bob has gone off to shoot a Rough-legged Buzzard which Nilas knows of.

May 31st.—Bob brought back three eggs, but failed to shoot the Buzzard. It's getting awfully hot. The water even in the fell streams is quite warm, and insects of all sorts are swarming. I got a lot of eggs of Brambling and Mealy Redpole to-day, also some Waxwings, and a Pine Grosbeak. One's time indoors is so much taken up with blowing and marking, one has scarcely any time to write a diary.

June 1st.—A man brought in to-day, an egg, which he swore was a Tengmalm's Owl's. He had taken it from a Golden Eye nest-box, and had, he said, seen an Owl come out. But it is evidently a diminutive Golden Eye's egg, as its colour and hard shell testify. Another man this evening brought in a clutch of eight Duck's eggs taken from a tree. The bird, he says, was white, and there are certainly numerous white feathers among the down, which he fortunately brought with the eggs. The House Martins are simply swarming.

I got a splendid clutch of five Tengmalm's Owl's eggs all containing embryos, two fairly large ones. One of the eggs is much bigger than the rest, almost the size of an Hawk Owl's egg. The rest was in an old stump not five feet high, open at the top, which I had noticed one and a half month's ago.

I find we have altogether now :—

117 skins.
1232 eggs.
7 skeletons.
3 skulls.
56 embryos in spirit.

Every individual skin, egg, and embryo numbered and marked—pretty good work.

The sun now appears to go just below the mountains, and I'm sure that on the top fells one would see the midnight sun. It is light enough now all night to shoot or write.

The man from Sirkojärvi came to see us to-day, and he says he knows of a Capercailzie's nest. He told us when we were there that on a certain hill Woolley had taken a Golden Eagle's nest, but they had not had eggs this year as far as I could understand. Finnish seems a most difficult language to pick up, perfectly different to most Western European languages, much more like Greek. All I can say are a few words, and fewer sentences. I found four Reed Buntings' nests to-day.

June 2nd.—Some of the Drakes are collecting on the river. This evening I saw a flock of twenty Pintail Drakes, and several lots of three or four Widgeon Drakes. These two Ducks seem to be the commonest about here.

I also twice to-day saw a Merlin; it seems curious I should not have found the nest. The people here distinguish between this and the Kestrel, and on two occasions eggs have been brought; I have been most careful in accepting them. They all say I shall get plenty later on. The pair I saw, if they were a pair, to-day, were not far apart, and one of them, when I climbed up a tree to a nest, made such a to-do screaming, I thought I was going to get some eggs. However, I shall go again next week and try, for Merlin's eggs from a nest in a fir tree would be curiosities, at any rate, in England.

Bob, this evening, caught twenty-three grayling which scaled $14\frac{3}{4}$ lbs., the largest being 2 lbs., all on the further bank of the rapid. The boys here snare lots of Ruffs on the shores of the bay, and keep bringing them in for us to buy, and some of them are beauties, but we haven't time to skin. The wind has changed to the North, and it is quite nice and cool. My little dog has got a sort of distemper, and looks on his last legs.

June 3rd.—The flies and midges are increasing to an alarming extent; this hot weather seems to have brought them out in millions. I caught several small frittillaries this afternoon, and a beautiful brown butterfly. I wish I knew which are rare and which are not.

I saw a Garden Warbler to-day. One ought to be able to extend the range of some of the Warblers. I should much like to take the nest of *Phylloscopus borealis*. There doesn't seem much chance of coming across any of the rarer Buntings. I went for a stroll this evening to try and find a pipe which I had left in the wood. I knew exactly where I had left it, but could not find the right track to the place. It must be very easy to lose oneself in these Lapp forests, and if it were not for the fell behind 'Niska, several times we would have lost our way. I saw another Skylark, evidently breeding here, and a Wax Wing, but could not find the nests.

Bob has been fishing up the river which comes from Onnasjärvi and caught forty-two grayling and seven trout—the largest 2½ lbs. The grayling were not so large. They were nearly all caught on a "teal and purple."

I have been out several times looking especially after Tits, as Wheelwright records the Marsh Tit at Quickiock. I suppose I have shot over a dozen here, all Siberian Tits, and have seen several close enough to be certain of their identity; so I feel pretty safe in accept-

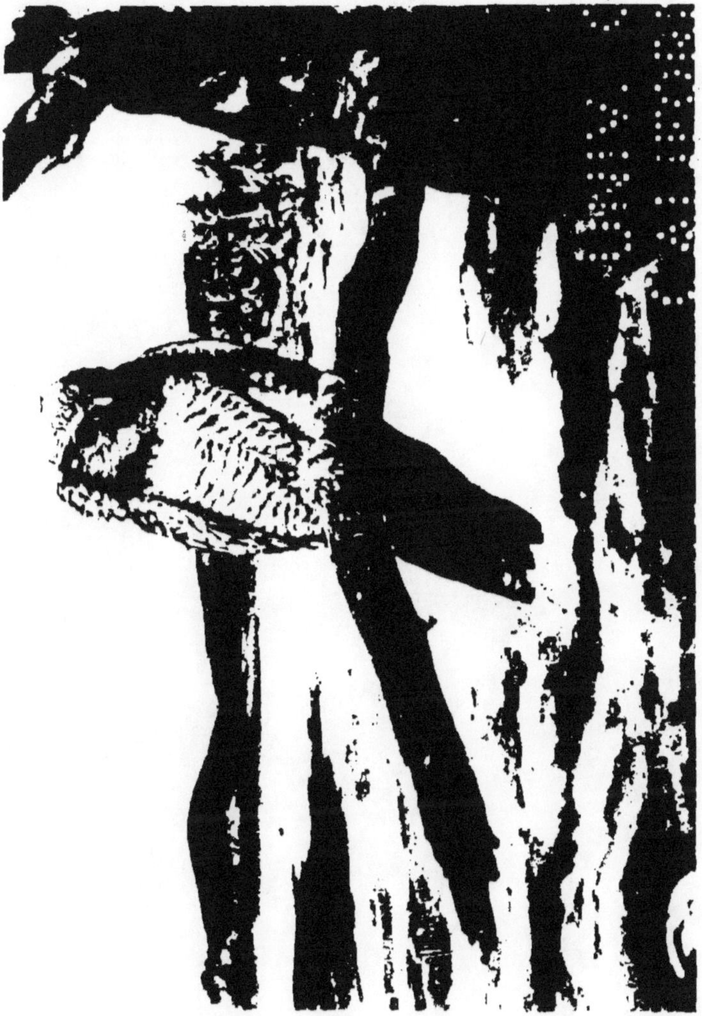

HAWK OWL.

ing Tits' eggs the boys bring in, particularly as the natives say they know no other.

June 4th.—To-day, a beastly wet day, I found nothing but a Brambling's nest in a fir tree, with one egg in. The Blue Throat, which does not appear to be common here, is called by the Lapps "Saddan Kiellinen," and by the Finns "Satagelinen." Both words mean "hundred tongues"—a name the bird well deserves.

A fish they catch here, which is very good to eat, called "süka," seems to be, excepting grayling, the fish of the place. Sükavuopio apparently takes its name from it. "The broadening of the river where süka are found."

June 5th.—A man brought in three hard set Wood Sandpiper's eggs, and on extracting the embryos I found an egg tooth on each mandible, which is curious. A boy also brought in some blue eggs, taken from a hole in a tree—the parent being black and white. They are certainly Pied Fly-catchers, since I have seen several about.

I am told there is no conscription here at Muonioniska, and no magistrate. The nearest place that has these luxuries is Kittila. They also tell me that two Lapps, who stole some reindeer, were sent off to Siberia, and when

I asked whether for life, the answer was "No, for 120 years." They must consider Lapps very long-lived.

We have both of us seen mountain hares in the "blue" stage. They seem to have changed very quickly since about a fortnight ago. The natives say that some years they are very plentiful. Evidently not so this year. At Quickiock, when Wheelwright was there, they were swarming.

The trout here are capital to eat, beautifully pink flesh, as good as Test trout, but we have them every day, morning and evening, and, as the alderman said, "toujours perdrix" becomes rather monotonous. We feed on Black Game, Willow Grouse, and Golden Eye eggs. The only thing to make it perfect would be some iced drink, as the weather is frightfully hot, and there is no night in which to keep away from the sun. We don't know when to sleep. As far as I can make out, we are out for about thirty-six hours, and then sleep for twelve, but it seems to suit us.

The Dusky Redshank I got to-day—I mean the eggs — I found on a dry patch of ground, where the heather had been burnt. The plumage of this bird—black and white—no doubt led it to breed there, which is very interesting, much more likely than the supposition that the bird assumed this particular plumage, since it began to breed in these particular places.

My dog Haali, was so ill to-day, and seemed to be in such pain that I thought it best to shoot him, which ceremony was performed behind the bread-house, and he was duly buried. Two other dogs have died in the village of apparently the same disease. He had not taken food of his own will for several days, and his eyes were terribly sunk in his head, and covered with film.

The cows aren't even let out of the stables yet. How an animal can live for more than half the year in the same stall I can't imagine.

June 6th. — To-day was quite a cold day, snowing hard in the morning. The change of wind seems to make all the difference, for when we have a south wind, the days are hotter than the hottest days in England, and the very next day it may be snowing.

A boy brought in three young Hawk Owls and the mother. They are ripping little birds, and I am having a cage made for them. They are apparently about ten days old, and covered with grey down, some of the wing feathers just appearing.

A man came in to-day and told me he had a lot of Haukka's eggs, which were taken four years ago in the neighbourhood, that year being a "lemming" year. I could not make out the bird he meant at all at first—smaller than an Eagle Owl — he called it "pikko nowkka ya," without ears, nesting in a tree, about the size of a Rough-legged Buzzard. On showing him Wheelwright's picture of a Ural Owl, he immediately recognised the bird, and said that he had seen none since. The eggs he possessed, which he says have full data, were ordered by someone who eventually did not take them—and he bought all the eggs he could that were taken in this valley—fifty-eight eggs in all—and he gave 2 kr. apiece.

It seems a curious fact that the more food there is about, the more eggs birds lay at a time. It is a well-known fact that birds of prey in "lemming" years lay many more eggs than usual, Snowy Owls, and Short-eared Owls laying eleven or twelve eggs in a clutch. Now, owing apparently to this year really swarming with insects, birds here are laying large clutches. I have taken Magpies with eight, Thrushes with six, and several other large clutches.

June 7th.—Snowing again, and very windy, the wind changing in the evening to North west; so we live in hopes of a fine day to morrow. In every clutch of pine Grosbeak's eggs, there appears to be one dull coloured egg, resembling that of a Blackbird, more or less, except being a little bluer. A full clutch seems to be five, sometimes four. There was a common Gull strutting about the village yesterday. I got the four Goshawk's eggs, taken at Hetta, to-day, which the man promised to bring. It seems curious that two birds so near akin as this bird and the Sparrow Hawk, should lay such different eggs.

June 9th.—On sexing a Dusky Redshank, taken on the eggs, I found it was a male. The eggs were almost hatching. I wonder if the male bird had performed the whole duty of incubation.

There are a lot of salmon jumping about in the rapids. We have seen the first Reeves about, yesterday and to-day; the Ruffs have apparently been here much longer than their mates.

To-day is Bob's coming-of-age birthday, and as it is becoming on such a day, we made it a record. The following is a list of what we obtained:

R. P. H.	87 grayling,	averaging	½ lb.
	6 trout,	,,	1¼ lb.
	2 perch,	,,	½ lb.

1 pike, averaging 1 lb.
1 Red-breasted Merganser.
1 Tufted Duck.
1 Mallard.
1 Widgeon.
1 Common Sandpiper.
1 Osprey.
8 and 12 eggs of Tufted Duck.

D. M. 1 Temminck's Stint.
2 eggs of Red-throated Diver.
4 of Kestrel.
8 and 4 of Redstart.
8 of Siberian Tit.

Brought in 5 and 5 Tufted Ducks' eggs.
2 Black-throated Diver's eggs.
2 Red-throated Diver's eggs.
2 Kestrel's eggs.
4 Dusky Redshank's eggs.
4 Wood Sandpiper's.
5 Mistle Thrush's.

Birds seen 5 Cranes.
2 Ospreys.
1 Golden Eagle.
1 Marsh Harrier.

Considering it was wet half the day, this is not bad and gives one a fairly good idea of what can be done up here with a rod and gun. Of course one could have shot any amount of the commoner Duck: one could any day—but rarity and variety is our object.

The Temminck's Stint is very common all along the shores of the bay, and I have several clutches already. They fly about, when the sun is shining, exactly like a Lark, hovering over places and uttering a twittering note, which is apparently kept up the whole time they are on the wing. They are absurdly tame, sometimes flying by within a yard, and settling close to one. They look scarcely bigger than the House Martins which fly about over the same area.

June 13th.—We spent the night on the marshes opposite the church, and birds of all sorts were swarming; Temminck's Stints, Wood Sandpiper, Ruffs, Reeves, Greenshanks, and Arctic Terns—all seemed to be screaming at the same time. We picked up a dead Red-necked Phalarope. This is the first we have seen so far. We each shot three Temminck's Stints and three Ruffs. The Temminck's Stints are extraordinarily tame, moving about like little mice in front of one, and one scarcely likes to shoot them, in fact it is pretty difficult to get far enough away. A Short-eared Owl flew over within shot early this morning. The young Hawk Owls are growing at an enormous pace, and seem most healthy. The feathers under the head have not yet begun to grow, and when they lift up their heads for food one sees a bare patch of skin under the chin. All the other feathers are in quite an advanced stage.

When I started for this place, I pictured to myself, during June, day after day without a cloud in the sky. The fact is, we haven't had a perfectly clear day since the snow left us.

Every Saturday night all the men and women go and bathe in the bay in front of the town, even the smallest children. They all run in perfectly naked and unashamed, and dip and run out. No one seems to be able to swim.

I took my skeletons from macerating yesterday, and hung them up to dry. They will, I think, be very good ones.

Now that the water has left the lowlands in the bay here, there is one huge swamp, not too bad to walk over, and we beat it last night for Ruffs and Sandpipers. If only one had it in England, I could not help thinking what a lovely place for Snipe it would make in the winter.

The first salmon was caught to-day in the nets, weighing 10 lbs., and on enquiring after it, we found it had already been sold to the postmaster, at 25 öre a lb.

June 14th.—We had arranged with a Finn who knew of a Rough-legged Buzzard's nest with young, to meet him to-day at Upper Muonioniska. We left 'Niska at 8.30, and after a pleasant row up the river of 8 miles, we arrived at his house. We saw several nice birds on the way, such as Rough-legged Buzzards, Ospreys, Scoters, Mergansers, etc. At his house we had coffee, and so we did at every house we came to on the way, two cups, making twelve each in all. After a walk of 5 miles over a hill, we arrived at the edge of a lake, perfectly mad with the mosquitoes, which seemed much worse to-day than they had been before, and, finding a boat, we rowed across. The scenery was beautiful, undulating country all around, covered with pines, the tops of the mountains alone being bare of trees, and down by the lake and along the river courses, birch trees. Pallastunturi, an enormous mountain some 25 miles away from 'Niska, looked grand in the distance, with the sun on it. Over the lake were flying all sorts of Ducks, particularly Golden Eyes, the males looking very bright in the sunshine, and over us screamed two or three pairs of those charming birds, which seem distributed all over this valley—the Arctic Tern.

I had fancied myself sitting in the boat returning to 'Niska, feeding three or four young Rough-legged Buzzards, but no such thing was in store for us; for at a Finn's house on this lake (there is one apparently on every fair-sized lake) one of the inmates informed us he had cut the tree down, killing the young birds. But our disappointment was more than partially dispelled, on hearing we were to be taken to an Osprey's nest. This proved to be some 15 miles off, on the way to Suontekio. We met the weekly post on the way, and tried to get our letters, but failed.

We approached the Osprey's nest, which was done very cautiously, as Bob wanted the male bird. As soon as it came in sight about 100 yards ahead, I fancied I could see the hen bird on the nest, and in a moment she slipped off and was far away on the lake. Bob in the meantime had gone some twenty yards ahead, and hid under a fir tree, while I and the guide also hid. The mosquitoes were awful, and after a minute, I was beginning to wonder how many more seconds the bird would be, as I could not stand them much longer. I was delighted to hear, after four minutes, a bang, and see the male bird come crashing through the trees close by. He had seen his mate slip off

SEA EAGLE.

the nest, and had not seen us, and wondering what was up, had flown up from the lake, looked into the nest, and sailed round over the tops of the trees, when he fell to Hornby's gun. The poor bird was only winged and defied us courageously. It seemed an awful shame to kill this bird with all his feathers on end, looking the picture of health and strength. The next thing was to procure the eggs. We had brought with us a wonderful climber. The tree was an enormous pine, and he could scarcely get his arms half way round, but he managed it, and after about ten minutes pulling away at the nest (these nests are so big, one can't get one's arms round them), he announced "kolme monat" (three eggs), and let them down in a stocking at the end of a rope; and lovely eggs they were, two of them unlike any I had got before. This is the fifth clutch I have taken up here. The nest was placed on an enormous pine, half-way up the side of a hill, overlooking the lake Nilimaajarvi. The bottom of the tree was strewn with sticks from the nest. All the Ospreys' nests I have seen up here, and I've seen a good many, including old ones, are always placed on the very top of a large pine, not always near the water. The base of the trunk of a tree holding a last year's nest, was not a foot from a fairly well-used track. The hen bird on this occasion kept circling round screaming occasionally, but at a considerable height, not protecting her nest with that courage which is attributed to her when her nest is robbed.

While we were sitting having coffee in a Finn's hut on the way back, a Short-eared Owl flew on to some sticks just outside. Here also we got a nest of four young pine Grosbeaks, fairly old. We arrived at Upper Muonio at about 2.30 and after coffee started down the river, with the sun shining, and very pleased. On the way down I took four Merganser's eggs under a small birch on the bank, so artfully concealed in the dead leaves, that unless it had been for old Laati, I never should have suspected one being there. We also took a single Sand Martin's egg.

The pine Grosbeaks are dear little birds, and make a call like "joey." They stretch themselves out in the sun with their heads lying over the side of the nest, and their crops distended, lying on the edge and supporting them. I never saw such greedy birds; with their mouths chock full they call for more, and scarcely take the trouble to swallow it when they've got it. We saw several broods of young Ducks, Tufted and Widgeon.

June 17th.—Bob caught to-day twenty or more grayling in the rapid of the big river. The five young Grosbeaks are doing fairly well on bread-crumbs, potato, rice, milk and berries. The young Hawk Owls also seem to be thriving.

June 18th.—There are fifty or sixty Arctic Terns flying over the large rapid below the town, hawking the flies floating down on the surface of the water.

We have Merganser eggs for nearly every meal now, and a nicer tasting egg one could not imagine. They are not half so strong in flavour as an English Duck's egg.

I've told all the people I want some Smew's eggs, and also that I'll give a good price for them; it's absurd the amount of variation these eggs seem to undergo, Tufted, Widgeon, Golden Eye, Merganser eggs are all brought in and asserted to be Smew's; but unless they bring in the old bird and the down, one cannot accept them. To-day, however, a boy brought six eggs out of a Golden Eye box, very like Widgeon, and these, though not authenticated, might be Smew's. Perhaps a microscope would detect them; of course the down could be distinguished as the Smew belongs to quite a different genus to Widgeon.

(On arrival in England the eggs were satisfactorily identified as those of Smews from the down.)

June 20th.—We bought a salmon to-day, about 7 lbs., and had him boiled for dinner. I shot an Ortolan Bunting. A flock of about twenty Cross Bill flew over me and I shot a young one. I expect they were all young birds, but this seems very early in the year for them to be flocking.

The weather is getting hot again, and the mosquitoes are awful. I only wish there was an entomologist up here collecting them.

June 22nd.—There's an awful mess on to-day. Nilas has brought in fifteen young Middle-spotted Woodpeckers. The brother has brought three young dead Rough-legged Buzzards, much too young to skin, and my spirit jars are full. The young Woodpeckers are making a dreadful noise, and it's pouring wet, so there's not much chance of getting food for them, and the young Hawk Owls are screaming for food too. There are about fifty eggs to blow, and another fifty to mark, several birds to skin, and it is as much as we can do to keep the boys out of the room, since the din of the Woodpeckers seems to attract them, and in the middle of it all the humourous postman, who will keep making jokes we don't understand, is trying to get more than 50 öre for three Whimbrel's eggs which he came across in the execution of his duties.

Last night we saw for the first time six or seven Swifts flying round the church steeple, but they are gone to-day.

I wish I had brought some more methylated spirits, since now the most interesting young birds are coming in, and my jars are chock full.

June 23rd.—To-day being beastly wet and cold we finished our packing, which was no small job, as either to-morrow or the next day, we expect Peter Johann, whom we told to come from Keniovuopio to fetch us. I'm only taking my bag and gun case, and an empty box for eggs, in case I get any on the way up, and my live birds. All the eggs (2,000), and skins, embryos, and skeletons, I'm sending down the river to Torneo by boat, thence to be shipped to England. I only hope they'll arrive before I do, or there'll be considerable anxiety. I'm almost ashamed of the quantities of birds' eggs I've taken. It looks as if I'd been robbing the country around of everything, but it is not so; I've found three times as many eggs as I've taken. I wish I had brought a Howard Saunders, as one never knows what is new or what is old. The Passerine Owl is an extremely rare bird. There is a pair about 14 miles from here, but we can't find the nest, though we've spared the birds. Siskins I don't believe come so far north.

I'm feeding the young Woodpeckers on ants' eggs, which they seem to enjoy—the boys collect them for me. They are all pretty old and can fly perfectly, and two or three are perfectly tame, taking anything out of my hand.

June 24th.—Peter Johann from Keniovuopio has arrived, with Mathias Johann (Sükarnopio), and Heinrich has agreed to take us up to Skibotten. Having finished packing, and having seen my eggs off to Torneo, we made ready to start. Just before this, however, a boy brought in three young Rough-legged Buzzards, which I put in the next divison of the cage to the young Hawk Owls.

We left at eight o'clock in the evening and many people came to see us off. The Finns have a curious way of shaking hands, one man with his right hand holds another's left shoulder, while the other touches with his left hand the other's right side.

We were much astonished at finding in our bill 160 kr. for the girl's wages, as she had never spoken about it before. However, we were very sorry to leave, and so were they apparently, to lose us. No doubt many people in 'Niska will be able to have such little luxuries as Singer's sewing machines with the few extra kroners we have left behind us.

Bob gave the boy his fishing rod, and we left many little things at the house, which they seemed to appreciate.

Leaving Upper 'Niska we encountered two rapids. The men are really wonderful at getting up these; two punt behind, and one in the bows, while we walk up the shore. Occasionally a tow-rope is used up the worst rapids. More birds seem to be found on the rapids than on the flat reaches of the river. Both the common Sandpiper and the Merganser abound on all the rapids, and we have shot several. The Merganser give capital shots; they come flying down at a great pace. The ones we kill are almost invariably males in full moult. Both this bird and the common Sandpiper are called in Finnish, after the rapids, koskilo and koski sippi. We also saw plenty of Divers of both sorts. The

Cuckoo appears to be most noisy during the light nights.

About midnight, a Great Grey Shrike flew across the river just in front of the boat. At about five o'clock in the morning, we arrived at Katkesuando, 21 miles from 'Niska. Here Bob shot a Short-eared Owl. We had a good sleep, and on waking in the evening, we found it blowing and raining, fairly beastly weather. Now we found our mackintosh rugs most useful in putting over the boxes and cages. I am sure no one, on such a trip, should be without something of the sort. Here I got a Mealy Redpole's nest — a perfect picture — lined with cotton grass, which grows in all the marshes.

Dan's diary ends abruptly here. He was too busy on the journey to Tromsö to continue it, and after he returned home, he was always intending to finish it from memory, but, somehow he never did.

R. P. HORNBY.

His friend, Mr. R. P. Hornby, has kindly filled in the remaining days of the journey over the fells, which reads as follows :—

By 8.30 we had packed the boat which was to take us up the river. The packing of the boat was a source of great anxiety to us, as it looked much too small to hold five men and all our luggage ; but we managed to get everything in at last.

The strongest of the three brothers was allowed about one square yard in the bows from which to do the poling ; then came my two boxes full of bird skins, and our portmanteau covered with bags of food, etc. With its back to this, was the cage containing three Hawk Owls and three Rough-legged Buzzards, and the cage with fourteen Woodpeckers on the top of it.

We were allowed about two feet of boat, in the middle, in which to stow our legs, while we sat on an empty box, which was for the eggs Dan might collect during his journey up the river. Behind us were the guns, etc., and all the small luggage. Then a small space in which Peter Johann might pole or paddle, and lastly the third brother with an enormous paddle, with which to steer.

By the time we had all got in, it was found that the gunwale was within 1½ inches of the water, and so the Finns lashed on wash-boards to keep the waves out when going up rapids; but we were so low in the water that it was always necessary for two or three of us to walk up the banks whenever we came to rough water, and we were never without the feeling that one mistake would mean the upsetting of all of us.

We started at about 8.30, after shaking hands with about fifty or sixty persons who had gathered to see us off, and, amid a chorus of good-byes (huversti), pushed off from the shore. The first 7 miles were easy going, as the water was sluggish, and so two or three of the Finns were able to scull us along, whilst we sat still and fed the birds. We started with some fourteen Three-toed Woodpecker, but only three survived until the third day, the others all dying of cold and hunger, and acting as food to the birds of prey, as soon as they had breathed their last. We were rather glad than otherwise when they were all dead, as they had to be fed with ants' eggs one by one, which took an enormous time, as ants' eggs were hard to get.

Upper Muonioniska was our first stop, but we only stayed there long enough to collect the eggs the people had ready for us, and drink a cup of coffee, and then on to Katkesuando, which we did not reach till the morning of the 25th, having taken a long time over the last 7 miles, which were nearly all rapids, causing Dan and myself to walk on the bank and drag the boat, with mosquitoes biting us all the way.

It began to rain heavily while we were unpacking the boat, so we decided to wait till it stopped. At the end of twelve hours it was still raining just as hard, and the river was beginning to rise, so we decided to push on, as Dan wished to reach Tromsö before Captain Schloshauer left, and I was anxious to get home as early as possible.

We had a very heavy bit of travelling for the next five or six hours, as the wind was bitterly cold, and the rain very persistent, so that the rocks by the side of the river got very slippery, and we stumbled along hour after hour, at one time towing the boat, at another hurrying on trying to shoot something for the Buzzards, which hardly ever stopped calling for food, no matter how much they got. Dan shot two Mergansers and one Diver. We stopped for an hour's rest at Savomiolka, and then on again for some six or seven hours, till we got to Palofoensi at about 10 a.m.

The 26th.—We decided to stop here for two or three hours' sleep as we were both pretty tired, and were rather amused when we walked into the hut to find ten men, all well-over six feet high, sitting in silence round the room, as we were accustomed to find two or three little Lapps in most of the huts. We sat in their midst for about an hour, when we were shown into another room, which had been got ready for us, and had a good sleep till 1.30, when we had some food and started for Kaaresuandro, some 35 miles on, and this took us some twenty-six hours' steady going, to accomplish. The weather had cleared by this time, and when the sun came out we were plagued by swarms of mosquitoes. The day's journey was without special incident, the same endless rapids, with an occasional bit of smooth water, so that we were employed most of our time in struggling over rocks or through swamps, while we towed the boat, which the three Finns poled from behind. We stopped once on the way, at Kuttainen, where we found some rather good eggs awaiting us, amongst which was a clutch of Broad-billed Sandpiper's eggs, and then on to Kaaresuandro, which we reached about 3.30 on the 27th. I managed to shoot one Scoter on the way, but we were again rather short of food for the birds as the last Woodpecker had been eaten. We were both so tired that

Dan decided not to look at any eggs till we had had some sleep, and it was some twelve hours later that the man woke us. The room was immediately filled with Finns and Lapps, of all ages and sexes, clamouring for us to look at their eggs, with the result that we had to clear the room partly by force, and partly by refusing to buy from them, except one by one. But even then it was impossible to look closely at all the eggs, and we must have refused many valuable ones.

Just before leaving Kaaresuandro we were surprised to hear someone address us in German. He turned out to be the priest's son, but his knowledge of German was very slight, so we did not gain much from our conversation with him. He was very much disgusted when we told him we must move on, as he hoped that Dan would stay and teach him English.

We started early on the 28th, and came across some Long-tailed Ducks. We also saw Ringed Plover, and one Buffon's Skua which we had not seen before. The journey, at first, was quite easy, as the country was flat, and we reached Mannu without having to tow the boat at all. This was the place where we had bought our dogs some three months before, and we were very sorry for the little children (who rushed out to see if we had their former pets) when we told them that they were both dead. We found only one good clutch of eggs here, Velvet Scoters, which were very acceptable.

We rested but a short time, as we had a long piece of river to ascend before reaching Sikavuopio. The sun was soon very hot, and the mosquitoes swarmed as usual. We spent an hour or two in crossing Lake Kellotigarvi, through which the river passed, and amused ourselves racing a little hunch-backed Finn, who paddled along behind us in his anxiety to reach his hut, in which he said there were lots of eggs waiting for us. When nearly across the lake we had a great piece of luck, as happening to pass close to the shore, we startled a Scaup Duck, whose nest Dan soon found, and he had the satisfaction of taking his first clutch of Scaup's eggs. We stopped for a few minutes, and boiled some coffee to celebrate this event, and then on to the hunch-back's hut at Vuokainem, where we got a few eggs, but nothing of great value. There was a very heavy rapid to get up immediately on starting, and Dan and I were forced to tow for two or three hours. We then walked ahead of the boat to try and shoot something for the

Hawk Owls and Buzzards, whose appetites were still growing. Dan managed to get a Capercailzie hen and three or four young birds, which we shared with the Buzzards.

We got to Sükavuopio just before midnight (there was no night), and found the place swarming with mosquitoes. This was just at the foot of an impassable rapid, and it was necessary to carry all our luggage three or four hundred yards overland to another boat, which was awaiting us at the top. Dan found a lot of eggs here, so that he was kept busy marking and packing them, whilst I skinned the Scoter and one or two other birds; so that we had very little sleep. We were surprised to find in the hut the names of several Russian officers who had been up the river, two years before, in order to observe the eclipse of the sun, and had brought a telescope with them, which must have been a difficult undertaking. One of the Finns had a photograph of them all muffled up in mosquito nets, so I do not suppose they enjoyed their observations much. We wrote our names under theirs on the wall of the hut to the great delight of the owner, who seemed pretty easily pleased.

On the 29th, we started to carry our luggage overland to the other boat, but the mosquitoes were so bad, that we soon gave it up entirely to the Finns, whilst we sat down with our veils on, endeavouring to avoid their bites, which got so bad that neither of us could speak from rage. When the changing of boats was finished, we wended our way, by easy stages, to Naimakka, where we stopped a short time for our usual cup of coffee, and then went all the way to Vittangi without a stop, some 20 miles, a good deal of it being rapids, which were getting much more difficult to negotiate now, as the river was narrower and steeper the nearer we got to its source. We found a woman in one of the huts, who had spent four years in England as cook. She spoke very good English, and seemed pleased to hear of England again. Dan gave her a silk handkerchief and one or two other presents on leaving. She was very useful to us, for by this time we had a huge stock of questions which we wanted to ask Peter Johann, but had been unable, owing to our limited knowledge of the Finnish tongue. At Vittangi we found the owner of the hut anxiously awaiting us. He had a lot of Rough-legged Buzzards eggs for Dan, and some Red-throated Pipits. He was delighted with the money Dan gave him for the eggs, as had been all the people up the river, and no doubt he must have thought us mad to give so much wealth for useless egg shells.

As far as we could judge this was July 1st, but we had been getting hopelessly lost as to the days, for the sun never set and it was hard to know always where the north was. Now that we were getting near the sea, we were getting more and more anxious to hurry on and catch the earliest steamer from Skibotten, which only ran twice a week, so we had but a few hours' rest and then started again for Keniovuopio, Peter Johann's home. We kept on steadily till we got to Vittangi, the home of the Graffers who were the other family of famous boatmen on the river; one of them came on with us in order to help us across the lake behind Peter Johann's home, and to pick up some ponies which were at another hut north of Keniovuopio. The going was terrible after we passed Vittangi, and it was impossible for Dan and myself to go in the boat at all. We towed till we came to an impassable rapid, where we had to unload the boat and carry the luggage half a mile over the swamps. We spent several hours at this game as we had to make three or four journeys each, whilst the mosquitoes had a glorious feed on our unprotected faces. We then had to get the empty boat up the rapid. Dan and I, and Peter Johann went on ahead with a long rope which we wound round a rock. One of the Finns went in the boat with a long pole to keep the stern clear of rocks, while the third man tied a pole to the bows of the boat and, walking along the bank, kept her from getting smashed against the side of the fall. We had to keep pulling in front all we knew to keep the bows of the boat out of the water. We did not envy the Finn in the boat, but he did not seem to care a bit, and poled away like a man, with the water rushing past him. We got the boat up at last almost full of water. It was fairly easy after this; the only difficulty being the want of water in places where the river broadened out. We reached Keniovuopio at about seven o'clock on the evening of the 1st. It was our intention to have about twelve hours' sleep here, so Dan told the Finns not to wake us till ten the next morning. I immediately went to sleep, whilst Dan sat up, blowing and marking eggs, seemingly still untired. He must have gone to sleep about 9.30. However, I woke up at ten o'clock, and seeing that it was ten, I immediately woke up Dan, as I thought it was ten the next day. He went to wake the Finns up and it was not till we had gone two or three hours on our journey that we discovered our mistake. We had started on the evening of the 1st instead of the morning of the 2nd. The Finns only thought we had changed our minds, and so had not said a word. We had but a few miles to go, when we arrived at the place where the ponies were, which were to carry our luggage over the mountains.

Soon after leaving the ponies, we came to the source of the river, where it came out of a lake; the boat had to be taken overland, and the luggage carried as before; but we had three ponies to help us this time, so Dan and I went and fished, leaving the Finns to do the work. It was the best bit of fishing I ever had. We waded on to a rock and in about nine casts I landed seven grayling weighing 18lbs, nearly 3lbs each. We then went higher up and I got six trout, best fish 2½lbs. They were very welcome indeed as articles of food, and we had a rare feast on the edge of the lake before starting on our last journey in the boat.

Lake Kilpisgarvi is almost like two lakes, as a very narrow channel divides the two halves. We rowed for 10 miles up the south shore, and then swam the ponies across the narrow piece to continue their journey on the north side of the lake.

We stopped at a little island at the end of 10 miles, and cooked our remaining fish. It had been raining for the last hour or two, and we were so cold and miserable, that we took off all our clothes and dried them in front of a roaring fire which the Finns made for us, though it was raining all the time. We also drank our last drop of brandy, which I think saved my life, for I was so cold from sitting in the wet boat, that I am sure I could not have survived the last 15 miles of lake, but for it. Lake Kilpisgarvi is 1,350 feet above the sea level and well in the Arctic circle, so it is terribly cold there when the wind is in the north. We got over the last 15 miles somehow, though we were nearly swamped all the way, and then there was only 45 miles of mountains to cross before we reached the sea. We did 20 miles that night, and did not stop till we reached Heligscoran, well over the top of the pass. I have but a hazy recollection of that last 20 miles of mountain climbing till we came to Skibotten. We each carried something on our backs and trudged on in silence, each anxious to be the first to reach Heligscoran. We forded two rivers which were running the other way down to the sea, and as both were very flooded it was dangerous work.

D. M.

LITTLE AWKS.

The ponies were of great assistance as we could hang on to them and trust them to find the shallowest part. We got to Heligscoran, at last, on the afternoon of the 3rd of July, quite tired out. I went to sleep as usual, but Dan was kept up marking and packing more eggs which were waiting for him in the hut. He was repaid for his work, as he got several of his best butterflies outside the hut. He had determined to wait till he got to the sea before he went to sleep, so whilst I slept, he looked for moths and butterflies, getting five which I think we had not got before. We started again for the sea that same evening on the last 25 miles of our journey. It was still raining heavily but we did not mind that, and loaded as we were, we almost ran down hill, so eager were we to see the sea. We did the first 15 miles without a stop, had a cup of coffee, and then finished the last 10. We reached the sea at about 2 a.m., on July 4th, three hours before the steamer started, and if it had not been for our curious mistake at Keniovuopio, we must have missed the boat.

We had been travelling for eight days and nine nights with never more than two or three hours sleep out of twenty-four, with the exception of our long sleep at Kaaresuandro.

We had come 200 miles up the river, and 60 miles from the top of the river, so that we had averaged over 30 miles a day. At Skibotten we paid the Finns, and gave them our rugs, etc., and everything we could spare, and then took a most affectionate leave of them. It was quite touching to see how grateful they were to us for having come to their country, and how sorry they were to part with us.

As soon as we got on board the steamer we went to sleep, and except for one or two meals we slept the whole forty-eight hours to Tromsö.

On reaching Tromsö, Dan sent off a characteristic telegram home to announce the end of his adventures and his speedy arrival in England. "From the luxury of Lapp, to the *lap* of luxury.—Dan." His boxes of skins, embryos and eggs, that had been dispatched down the Muonio arrived three weeks after we did, and so well were they packed that out of 2,482 eggs, only one was cracked and none were broken.

MOTTISFONT ABBEY. M. K. W.

THE MOTTISFONT BIRDS

AND

THEIR MASTER.

One of the best managed, and one of the largest collections of living eagles and raptorial birds in this country, is at Mottisfont Abbey, on the Test, near Romsey. The Abbey, or rather the fine Tudor house, built by Lord Sandys on the site of the Abbey, is the residence of Mr. Meinertzhagen; the eagles and other birds were obtained, and the aviaries designed and their excellent management devised by his son, Dan Meinertzhagen, whose regretted death, at the age of twenty-three, took place on February 13th, 1898. His birds and collections are still maintained as he left them. At the present time there are sixteen eagles in the houses, with some kites, buzzards, and other hawks. The collection of owls, great and small, is quite as fine as the eagles, and gives a second line of interest to this unique set of private aviaries. It may be asked, what is the distinction of this special collection, and in what does it differ from that of the Zoo? The answer is that here only in this country can these, the finest of all birds, be seen in the health and vigour which nature gave them.

The eagles look what they are, the kings of birds. There is not a starve mark, and hardly a broken feather to be seen in their plumage; their eyes are bright and keen, and they have no disease of the feet and toes, and every bird looks, and is, ready to fly and catch its prey if it were let out to-morrow. Some of them have flown loose about the Abbey for months before being confined to their cages.

We propose to say something of the founder of this collection, of whom, since his days at Harrow, it is difficult to say whether animals of all kinds had more fascination for him, or he for them. His room there always contained a small menagerie, such as a couple of dab-chicks in a bath; some young jackdaws in his Sunday hat; a squirrel, and a family of dormice in the curtains; whilst in the garden were his eagles.

The idea of forming a private collection of living eagles and raptorial birds was original, and its success beyond expectation. But no description of the birds, as they are seen to-day, would be complete without some reference to the author of the undertaking. There is little doubt that when Dan Meinertzhagen died, we lost a mind almost perfectly equipped by nature to make a mark amongst those best fitted both to learn

and to set out, in its most attractive form, the modern study of the life and history of birds. Without in the least exaggerating what he did, or mistaking promise for performance, we may, without hesitation, set down the names of Audubon, Wolf, and Seebohm, as those with whom his work (if it had been maintained) would have entitled him to rank in the future: Audubon, because his gift for painting and drawing birds was developed even earlier than it was in Audubon, and also because he was a first-class field naturalist; Wolf, because, in painting birds his knowledge of their daily life and sense of colour and pictorial effect was of the same kind, and the results he had already produced were such as delighted that veteran animal painter himself, of whom Landseer declared that "Before he was a man, he must have been an osprey;" and Seebohm, because he had the same gift for original observation in new and distant regions.

It is a thousand pities Dan Meinertzhagen did not live to finish the monograph on "The Eagles of the World" which he began at the age of seventeen. In the exquisitely written pages of this book, the young author set down the most minute facts, gathered from the notes of naturalists the world over, concerning these birds, illustrating the type with charming little pen and ink vignettes drawn either from life, or from good pictures he had access to. The buzzard here shown, drawn after Thorburn's picture, is one of the illustrations of the MS; other illustrations in this book, are taken from the same book. The beautiful and minute handwriting, portions of which are shown in some of the illustrations, written on folio sheets, is striking enough in itself. The pages are without blot or erasure, written with the effortless precision which marked all his drawings. When a small boy of eleven he copied Doyle's frontispiece of *Punch* so accurately, that it might be mistaken for the original leaf torn off; and in a scientific monograph on "Owls," by Mr. W. P. Pycraft, just published by the Linnean Society, will be found other examples of the same exquisite draughtmanship, done in Professor Lankester's laboratories at Oxford. This incomplete history of eagles and hawks, contains many drawings as life-like and as accurate as those here reproduced; and the sketches not finished betray no sign of the amateur, though begun when he was a boy.

Several of his original sketches in water colours are reproduced in these pages. The two Little auks, playing on the sea, were drawn from one little bird picked up in the Oxford meadows during a storm, and allowed to disport itself in the undergraduate's bath, and so the two positions were secured that made the picture. The Golden-eagle is one from St. Moritz ; and the Spotted-eagle is his old Harrow favourite, that flew free about Mottisfont for some time. It would wing its way right across the Test valley to a large "Scarr" of bare chalk cliff on the downs opposite, returning every evening to be fed at the aviaries.

At the age of ten Dan made a rare collection of British wild flowers, only to be succeeded the next year by an equally good one of butterflies and moths. He set his butterflies beautifully. The caterpillars, and how to preserve them, bothered him for some time, until he learnt from Mr. Meek, the Naturalist, the art of "rolling them with a pencil"—blowing them out, and arranging them in natural positions. This mode of death, at first, rather shocked his kindly nature. "But how do you *kill* them ?" said the boy. "*Kill* them?" said the naturalist, "there is'nt much life left when their insides are out." A year or two later Dan had the satisfaction of teaching this method of preserving caterpillars to Mr. Henry Elwes, a well-known entomologist, and in return was told how to catch a purple emperor with a bit of raw meat. As luck would have it, the chance of trying the bait came early one morning when the boy saw from his bed a purple emperor fluttering about on the top of a plane tree outside his window. He was down in the larder, in his night shirt, in half-a-minute, hacking at a leg of mutton for the necessary meat, and before ten minutes had passed he rushed triumphantly into his mother's room with the captured butterfly. Birds and their eggs succeeded butterflies, and, in these, Dan found an inexhaustible pleasure both in collecting, in drawing, and in studying their habits.

His home at Mottisfont Abbey made an ideal headquarters for his pursuits. The river Test, divided into two streams, with an intervening marsh, duck ground, and heronry, is full of wild birds and water fowl, and there was ample scope for aviaries, and for keeping large birds free and wild about the place. The story of these makes a more direct appeal to most readers than the more serious side of his work, and the management of his birds, both in the aviaries and out-of-doors, was so clever and thorough, that it has the intrinsic interest which can be claimed for any pursuit which is done as well as it can be, especially when the difficulty of keeping these large carnivorous birds in health is realized. He had two Sea-eagles, which were loose about the grounds for three months. They became almost too bold and tame. Though they made their head-quarters at the house where they were fed, they made long flights up and down the river and water meadows, fed on trout and other fish, and took toll of the chickens at the farm, and cats, wherever they found them. The chicken yard was not far from their aviaries, outside which they were fed. The cats they picked up where they could. They even chased the prize pussy belonging to a lady who lived near; but this cat escaped. One of their oddest feats was that of robbing a gentleman who was fishing in the river near. He had just landed a fine trout, and was extracting the fly from its mouth, when something like a dark cloud came over his head. It was one of the eagles, which swooped down on him, seized the trout, and flew off with the fish, the line, and the top of the rod. He said it made him feel nervous for the rest of the day. One of these eagles flew fifteen miles off, to Salisbury where it was shot. The other was caught and put in the aviary. When loose the eagles roosted mainly in the great plane tree near the river. They would even threaten to attack small dogs, and there is little doubt that had they had the chance of pouncing on them quietly, with no one near, they would have done so. One motive for confining the survivor was the fear that it might possibly attack small children.

Among other birds kept in these early days was a Raven named "Jacob," this was among the most intelligent of all the Mottisfont pets. He was passionately fond of his master, and would sit on his shoulder "cooing" at him like a pigeon, follow him wherever he went, and was intensely jealous of any other animal he liked. He hated any dog, or other bird he petted. Among these was a kite, whose food Jacob always stole. They were then given separate meals on separate lawns, on either side of the house. When Jacob found this out he would bury his dinner quickly under some leaves, and fly over to the kite and steal his food. A long course of low diet reduced the kite's strength, until he could not fly, when Jacob saw his opportunity—he seized the kite by the scruff of the neck, dragged him to the river side and drowned him. Jacob kept a

JACOB.

DAN AND JACOB.

regular larder under some leaves in a clump of trees, so he was never at a loss for food. Once the old dandie Roddy found this hoard of food and devoured it. When Jacob discovered his loss he gave a furious croak, and came out of the clump like a demon possessed, and literally rolled over and over on the ground in helpless rage. Many a nip did Roddy get to his tail to punish him for his theft. Jacob was a rare rogue, and led the gardeners a dance by pulling up any plant he saw them put into the ground. He had to be locked up during the bedding-out season. He would stand at a respectful distance with his head demurely on one side, watching their operations, but no sooner had they gone off to dinner than every plant was quickly plucked up and laid on its side, and Jacob back again on his bough, pruning his glossy blue feathers as if nothing had happened.

Jacob's death was a terrible tragedy. He liked to go out shooting with his master, and one day, accompanied him to a covert two miles off. There, towards evening, he was lost, and did not return that night. Next day he went into a village, and seeing a woman in the road, hopped up, and began to pull at her dress, as was his custom when asking for food at Mottisfont. She said she thought it was "the devil himself," and being frightened, called to a man, who, with incredible stupidity and callousness, fetched a gun, and shot the poor raven in the road.

Dan had a pair of Cormorants, all one summer, which soon became ridiculously tame. There is a smooth turf slope from the lawn to the main drawing-room window. Up this the cormorants would walk, and were sometimes found, most unwelcome guests, sitting on the backs of the drawing-room chairs, and refusing stoutly to be evicted. They soon cleared off some of the stock of fish in that part of the the river which runs close by the Abbey.

The Vociferous Sea-eagle from Senegal, whose portrait both in pen and ink and water colour are here, was a great favourite of its master and has often been taken for an airing about the grounds on his arm. It has lived six years at Mottisfont, and is a most beautiful creature, with a white head and breast, a bright chestnut belly, and back of slaty blue, with chestnut trimmings. It is very tame and fearless. All the portraits here given of the eagles, other than those from drawings by their owner, show the birds with leather "jesses" on, like hawks, evidence in itself that they could all be handled and treated as semi-tame birds. The secret of the health in which the whole collection is maintained, lies partly in the construction of the cages, and partly in the food given to the birds. Anyone who desires to keep even a single eagle in captivity should examine the Mottisfont cages. They are divided into front and back chambers, but the latter are partly dark and so screened from the outside view, that the bird can secure absolute quiet if it desires it. It is also sheltered from cold, wet, and wind. Outside, instead of having the damp ground as the floor of the cage, the eagles live above a wooden platform set 3½ feet from the ground. This platform is dry and solid, and allows no damp to lie on it. The eagles consequently do not damp their wing and tail feathers, or contract cramps and chills as they would on cold concrete. Above this are perches of natural branches, and on these the eagles sit sunning themselves, and surveying the charming landscape sloping down to the Abbey and across the wide valley of the Test. On a stormy day they may be seen, for hours together, with out-stretched flapping wings, screaming at the pitch of their voices as if they well understood what a joy it would be to them to sail off into the unknown world beyond.

Three White-tailed Sea-eagles are now in the aviaries. One of these birds is unquestionably the finest and largest captive eagle in this country. It is a female, taken from a nest in Lapland. In size and bulk she is one-third larger than the other pair, though these are fine specimens. The head, seen from the back, looks as broad as a bull-terrier's, and at a guess her weight must be 16lbs. at least. She is very savage, and "goes for" her keeper, who nevertheless catches her, and holds her up by the legs like a giant turkey, on a plan for handling eagles devised by her young owner. The man approaches quietly, suddenly throws a baize cloth over her feet, and then seizes the legs through it.—Dan was an adept at the handling of these large birds of prey, and only once did he have anything like a bad accident with one. He was taking his spotted-eagle out for an airing at Harrow when the bird returning to perch on his arm, which was covered with a long leather gauntlet, came down with such a swoop that it missed the arm and clutching at the side of the leg, tore down his trouser and dug his talon through a thin leather boot, into the instep and lamed its owner for some days. It was a sight to see Dan go into the large aviary

THE AVIARIES. MOTTISFONT

where the three Sea-eagles live. The whole place seemed alive with wings, beaks and talons, and yet never an inch did Dan move to avoid them. He was once chaffed by one of his cousins, who is a good man across country, about not caring for a mount to hounds; but the tables were turned when the said cousin was taken into the aviary, and made himself very small in a corner imploring to be let out again from "those horrid birds." Dan had no idea of a horse except as a means of locomotion. He would leave the reins on the animal's neck and let it go it's own pace. Once he was minded to go out with the New Forest Hounds on his sister's horse, rather a hot little thoroughbred. What they said *of* him and *to* him had better not be recorded; but as he described his day, "Oh yes, it was splendid. I rode in front of everyone, hounds and fox included. Splendid exercise! I feel quite stiff, and Astor too seems to have had quite enough of it."—When these eagles were loose in the poultry yard, they were caught by throwing sacks over them whilst feeding on some luckless hen. The illustration gives some idea of the head of the Sea-eagle, but does not indicate by any contrast her extraordinary size. Her wings are over

9 feet across. She is as large as the Stellar's Sea-eagles at the Natural History Musseum.

Bonelli's eagle, of which an illustration is given, came from Spain. It is a long-legged species, with a small head and large talons. This bird was kept at Oxford and partly trained to be flown at rabbits like a goshawk. As eagles are regularly trained by the Kirghis to take small deer in Central Asia, and occasionally to help in wolf hunting on the Steppes, this experiment would very probably have succeeded.

There are two Golden-eagles, one from Austria and the other from Morocco. One bird has been four years at Mottisfont. A pair previously in the collection, were sent from St. Moritz to Harrow, where their owner had an aviary, when a boy, in Mr. Bushell's house. They arrived on a Sunday morning during chapel time, and were unpacked after Service before an admiring congregation.

One Wedged-tailed eagle came from Australia. These birds are believed to have the finest powers of flight even amongst eagles. They have extraordinary long legs and talons, and the eagle at Mottisfont *runs* in the most amusing and agile manner. The plumage is much coloured with a bright russet brown.

DAN AND EAGLE AT HARROW.

When on the perch it droops it's wing *always*, as if the muscles of the lower parts were too heavy, except when used in flight. Among trained hawks this drooping of the wing is considered a sign of an ill-tempered bird. In the illustration, the bird is angry and alarmed. When quiet she has a smooth snake-like head and neck. A dark-coloured Imperial-eagle from Spain was brought into the collection in 1896. Some of these birds were companions of the Harrow days. Mr. Bushell, his house master, kindly allowed an aviary, for a certain number of eagles, to be constructed in his garden, and the perseverance with which Dan maintained his birds under all the disadvantages of school life is remarkable. Here is his portrait as a boy, in his Harrow hat and coat, with his spotted-eagle; the bird is sitting for its picture quite obediently.—A funny little story is told of these Harrow days. Dan and his brother were collecting birds eggs and skins together. They secured from Scarboro' a somewhat rare bird, and could not come to an agreement as to its proper name. They heard that a certain distinguished Professor was staying with one of the Harrow masters, so the two boys rushed over with their skin to beg him to decide the difficult question, and waited with bated breath for his decision. After a cursory glance the great man said, "It is a *so and so.*" The name of the bird is forgotten. "Oh no!" exclaimed one of the boys, "we *know* it isn't that. We are only in doubt if it is a *so and so*, or a *so and so.*" "Well my boys," said the kindly Professor, "you seem to know a good deal more about it than I do; but if you like, I will take the skin up to the Natural History Museum and get it classified for you." And so he did, telling the boys after that it was one of the birds they had disputed about. — At Oxford, life was different. He was able to give as much time to his pursuits as he wished, and had hosts of friends who were not only very devoted to him, but shared his pursuits. He studied those branches of science needed for his work on ornithology, in which his power of accurate drawing was of great service. A specimen of drawing in anatomical work is given opposite.

A Tawny-eagle, two Spotted eagle, and a Chilian-eagle, all occupy one large cage at Mottisfont. These birds live in quarters originally designed for the "poor leopard" which was burnt at Oxford. According to the keeper's account "Mr. Dan" smuggled him into college in a portmanteau. An Oxford

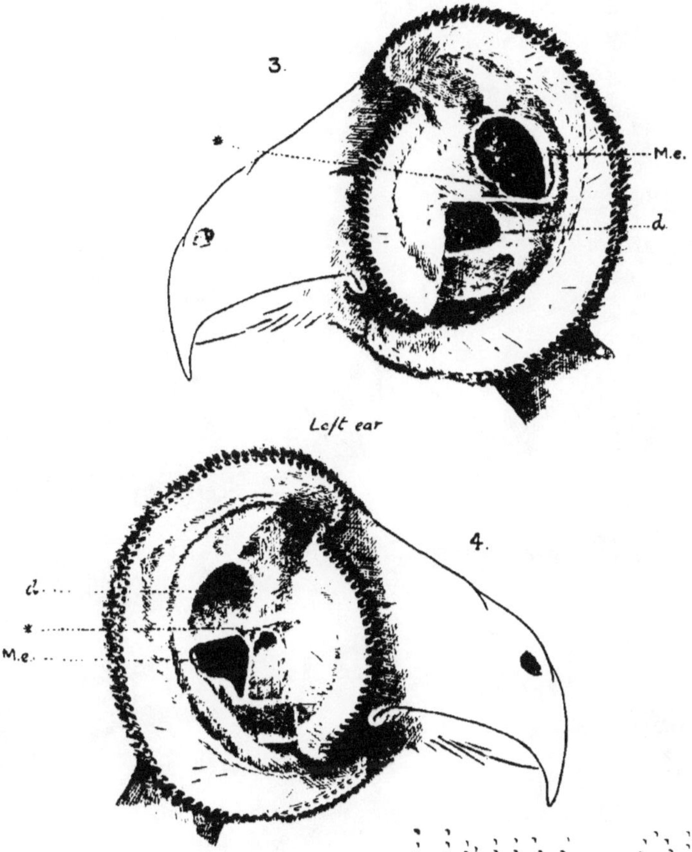

Right ear

ASIO ACCIPITRINUS

STUDIES OF OWLS EARS.

DRAWN FOR THE LINNEAN SOCIETY.

friend assures the writer that this was a most attractive little cub at New College. He lived for some weeks in his master's rooms, sleeping in his bedroom at nights, as the scout would not enter the sitting room with the leopard alone there. Dogs are forbidden in college; but this animal coming under the category of cats, there was a good deal of discussion with the authorities, before he received his final notice to quit. He was placed in an out-house; but unfortunately when the cold weather came, and an oil stove was provided to keep him warm, he upset the stove and burnt both himself and his home, much to the grief of his master, who had just proposed bringing him home for the Christmas holidays as a playmate for his small brothers and sisters.

The dog "Pita" was the leopard's successor in the New College rooms. Her portrait is shewn here with the Dandie, and one of Dan's small sisters. Independent of nature, and rather surly to strangers, Pita's devotion to her master, and indeed, to every member of his family, was all the more striking. Like the leopard, she was forbidden in college; but in his rooms she lived for several terms without ever entering in at the door. Dan had taught her to jump several feet across a deep area, on to a sloping window-ledge and so through a narrow casement window into his room. She would leave her master quite contentedly at the New College gate, and by the time he arrived in his room, Pita would be sitting by the fire waiting for him, with a broad grin on her face, much to the astonishment of any visitor who happened to be with him. This feat nearly cost Pita her life once. Unfortunately when she landed on the steep ledge outside it was only to find the casement shut, and it was all she could do to turn round and jump back through the railing.

The periodical arrival of a family of pups was a sore trial to Pita's affection for her master, and also to her temper; as long as the pups were kept in their box or tub, Pita felt it her painful duty to remain with them; but she would give an occasional rush to the house just to see that Dan was still there, and woe betide any man or boy who chanced to be near as she passed between her two attractions. She was so savage at these times to all that were not of her master's family, that after a week or so, the pups had always to be destroyed, some day during her absence. When she returned and found her family gone, and her maternal cares ended, she would scamper

wildly off, a free creature again, able to devote her whole attention to the one she loved best. On one occasion Dan left Mottisfont a few days after the pups had been drowned, and Pita was much exercised in her mind as to whether she had done wisely to be pleased at her puppyless condition. After a little she decided that her tub was rather desolate, and with a curious working of the canine mind, she fetched four dead moles that were hanging on a railing near, and put them in the place of her pups, and she soon became as ferocious over these treasures, as if they had really been her progeny. For months after Dan's death, if Pita heard a lively air being played on the hall piano after the manner of her master, who was an accomplished musician, she would look up in a curious quick way, and dash off to see if it could possibly be him come back again—but alas! to return in a few seconds, with a disappointed expression on her face. I am sure if she could speak, she would oftentimes have said, "Where is he? that he never comes back again."

Dan's collection of owls, which supplements that of eagles, was largely made during the last two years of his life. The Milky eagle-owls from Benin, as shown in the picture, were two out of three brought back after the Benin Expedition, and are the only specimens in Europe. One was destined for St. Petersburg, but Dan managed somehow to stop it on the way, and change its course to Mottisfont. Their lichen-coloured grey plumage is set off by great black eyes and heavy eye-lids of what looks like russet leather, and gives them an air of extraordinary intelligence. They are perfectly tame and fearless, not moving even when strangers touch their cage. They only eat at night. There are Burrowing owls, which constantly make new holes and breed every year. The set of Eagle-owls, of which the Benin owls are the African representatives, is made up by a splendid pair of European eagle-owls, taken from a nest on the rocks near Tromsö, with cairn gorm coloured eyes; and exquisitely marked Virginian eagle-owls; the plumage of these is all coloured horizontally, with dark grey on silver ground, and is exactly like the bark of the silver birch.

The Brazilian wood-owl, as shown in the slight water-colour sketch, was a very comical good-tempered bird. He loved to have his head scratched, and directly his master approached his cage, would ruffle up his feathers and stretch out his neck to be patted. He was a greedy contented little person, and although he was christened the "Dancing Master," he never budged off his perch except at the sight of food. He died from overfeeding.

Four little Scops' owls were very quaint dainty little birds. When at rest, with their feathers tightly pressed against their sides, as in the pen and ink sketch, and eyes nearly closed, they looked exactly like part of the bough they perched upon. They were very shy, and when frightened would dart like a silent flash into their holes, but only to put an inquisitive little head out in a few moments to see if the coast was clear.

The little Pigmy-owl was a sweet little creature. The smallest of his species, his proper food is insects. It was difficult to find him the diet he liked in the winter. Getting the right food for each bird was an endless work and pleasure to their master. A large colony of white rats is kept close to the aviaries, and whenever a bird is sick or sorry, one of these is killed and given, quite fresh, to the invalid, and if anything will cure him, it is this great delicacy and natural food. Scores and scores of pike have been wired out of the Test and given to the sea-birds. The excitement that the sight of a whole fresh fish amongst them creates is most entertaining. The one who secures the dainty morsel spreads his wings over it in triumph, whilst the disappointed birds strut angrily around.

During a three months' sojourn at Gottingen, in 1894, it was not long before Dan provided himself with the inevitable eagle-companion, and he was soon known amongst the students there as the "eagle-man." His bird escaped one day and flew off into the country, with Dan and a dozen or so of German students in hot pursuit. After a ten miles' run across country the bird was marked down and secured. They all made for the nearest village, and hired an ancient chariot and four, and drove back to the university town, full of triumph, beer, and song. One of Dan's letters describing his first visit to a Gasthaus, to see some duelling, is interesting.

"I went early on Saturday morning to see the students of the University here fighting. I drove to a Gasthaus about a mile from the town, and sent in my card by the coachman (Baroness von K—'s factotum), and got him to explain who I was—I could not have done it well enough. As I was standing outside

D. MEINERTZHAGEN, 1897.

I saw a student sharpening his sword; only the tip is sharp, all the rest is blunt. I then walked in and was shown up into a gallery. All the students were sitting around drinking beer, except a few in the centre of the room. These were dressing up two men who were going to fight, putting pads over their mouths —they have to breathe through their noses— also pads over their necks, and goggles over their eyes, and their ears are fastened tight to their heads with a sort of glue. There had evidently been a lot of fighting already, as the floor was reeking with fresh blood, which has stained the soles of my new Peter Yapp two guinea patent leathers. Soon the whole assembly stood up, and the seconds shouted something which I presume meant "begin!" and then slash! slash! slash! only three cuts and all was over for the first round. They were immediately surrounded by their parties, each party wearing different colours, and their wounds were looked to, and, if necessary, were mopped up with cotton wool. Then another round—just two or three cuts at each other, all the work of a second, and so on till eight or nine rounds had been completed, and they were both streaming with blood. One of them nearly fell down, I suppose from loss of blood, just before the last round, and had to be propped up with a chair. They were then taken to a room to be doctored and washed. The others returned to their beer. All the glasses, tables, everybody, and everything, except a few up in what they were pleased to call the gallery, were covered with blood, and the floor was simply a duck-ground of blood. After that I walked through it, and managed to reach the door without fainting. The smell was something awful; I am sure I could not have stayed much longer without fainting or being sick. The smell and the heat were so awful—not the sight. I am accustomed to blood, at least birds' blood.

This is all contrary to law, of course, but the police must, I presume, half close their eyes. A certain Count H— has been very good to me; he has got me a Sparrow-hawk, and has asked me to play tennis to-morrow with two other Counts. Young Baron K— is back from London, he is awfully nice and very good to me."

The summer of 1892 was spent in Renvyle, in Ireland, by Dan and his younger brother Dick. Dan writes, August, 1892. "We are doing beautifully; yesterday we went out shooting in the bay, and got five Red-shanks, three Curlews, two Cormorants and one heron; I skinned them in the evening. The Cormorants were most unpleasant to skin. We drove here in a horrible thing, but quite the usual conveyance—we looked like this—

We shoot in the morning, and till three in the afternoon, then skin from three to ten p.m. I could feed two dozen eagles on the carcases of our birds. This is a ripping hotel: you can do whatever you like. There is a smoking room, where we go to clean our guns, and everything as in a country house. Young Mr. Blake told us any amount of boycotting experiences last night; how he and his mother were several times shot at, and a policeman killed. We had to get special licenses for carrying fire-arms in this parish. Mr. Blake had lunch the other day at the house of a man, and with two men, who had shot at him and his mother eight years ago.

Waiting for Curlew—

In January, 1898, Dan went to Bremen, where his grandfathers' ancestors had lived for nearly 300 years as burghers of the ancient Free Town. Hardly a week had passed before he had discovered the best naturalist in the place, a well-known German ornithologist. He writes to his father :—

"I got an introduction the other day to an old gentleman—Dr. Hartlaub—here, who knew your father and old Frederick Huth when he was a volunteer in some office over here. He is, I believe, the first ornithologist in Germany and is eighty-six years old. He has not seen Lord Lilford's plates of birds, so if you are going to Mottisfont at any time, pick out two or three parts, with *Thorburn's* pictures, not Keulemann's, and send them to me here. I'll be very careful with them."

On Wednesday, the 9th day of February, Dan was taken ill with what was at first considered only a slight indisposition. His wonderful good spirits and pluck, in bearing pain, deceived his doctor, and it was not till it was too late, and, indeed, only a few hours before his death, that the gravity of his illness was realized. He died early on Sunday morning, the 13th of February, 1898, after four days' illness of peritonitis. The personal charm that had endeared him to a host of friends, at college and elsewhere, augmented the general regret felt outside his family circle at his untimely death. Even on the river, the flag of the New College barge was flown half-mast high on the day of his funeral.

On his grave stone in the quiet little churchyard at Mottisfont, are written Coleridge's beautiful words, as suggested by his Harrow master, Mr. Bushell :—

" He prayeth best, who loveth best,
All things both great and small;
For the dear Lord, who loveth us,
He made and loveth all "

SOME PICTURES AND ETCHINGS

BY

DAN MEINERTZHAGEN.

BUZZARD—*After* THORBURN.

GOLDEN EAGLE.

D. M.

GOLDEN EAGLE.

D. M.

SPOTTED EAGLE.

D. M

GOLDEN EAGLE.

D. M.

BRAZILIAN WOOD OWL.

D. M.

BURROWING OWL.

D. M.

VERREAUX EAGLE.

D. M.

VOCIFEROUS SEA EAGLE.

D. M.

HOBBY.

D. M.

EAGLE OWL.

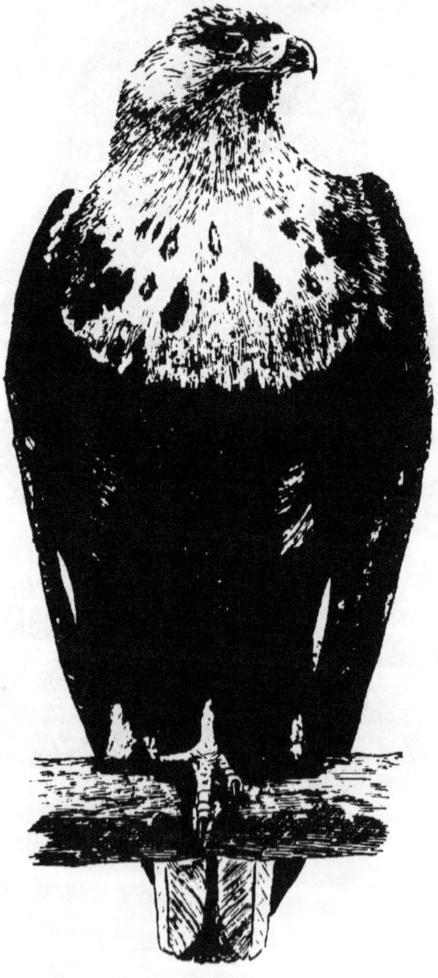

VOCIFEROUS SEA EAGLE.

D. M.

HOBBIES.

D. M

SCOP'S OWL

lagoons just behind Swatow on 20th March, 188? ...
coast in the beginning of February 1889, which ...
species to be the rarest of the Eagles of China ...

... n reptiles, especially on frogs. To...
... apparent, the birds being generall...

THE SPOTTED EAGLE.

From MONOGRAPH ON EAGLES—D M

HEN HARRIERS.

From MONOGRAPH ON EAGLES.—After Lodge

DEATH OF THE MALLARD

ıt along the ridge to the little
'l flakes of down. These eggs

Seebohm..

DEATH OF THE MALLARD.

From MONOGRAPH ON EAGLES

ed by Dr Lansdell from the Thian Shan moun-
k. Second Yarkand Mission. R.B.S p 7 (1891)
of Mont Vilan (7800), in the Grisons Specimens
e case containing two birds which were killed

Hotel, St Moritz,
near there; the
tria. D.M.
king
rock
alone
ture,
oc-
how-
ecies
ties-
hus
ral
e laid
ber,
The
kly
than
of
s of
bird
months

(from a photograph)

bed me
.B. Tristram. Notes on B. observed in S Palestine. Ibis
veds' by the 'weds' or mountain ranges of the les
aid to be gregarious, especially in the ...

GOLDEN EAGLE.

From MONOGRAPH ON EAGLES.

BENIN OWLS.

PIGMY OWL.

BONELLI'S EAGLE.

VIRGINIAN EAGLE OWL.

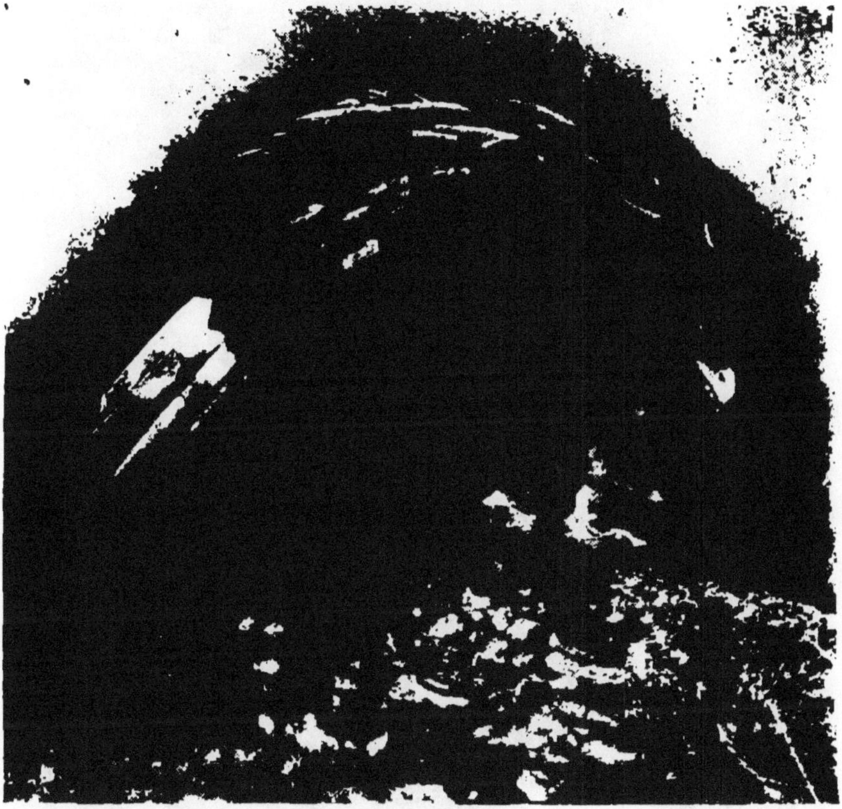

GOLDEN EAGLE.

TAWNY EAGLE.

BURROWING OWLS.

VOCIFEROUS SEA EAGLE.

www.ingramcontent.com/pod-product-compliance
Lightning Source LLC
Chambersburg PA
CBHW030831270326
41928CB00007B/996
* 9 7 8 3 3 3 7 0 9 5 3 3 8 *